KERRI

MW01673203

THE LAW FIRM GROWTH MACHINE

Revealing a PROVEN SYSTEM to ACCELERATE
Your Firm's GROWTH in Just 30 DAYS

KerriJames presents:

THE LAW FIRM GROWTH MACHINE

Revealing a Proven System to Accelerate Your Firm's Growth in Just 30 Days

Copyright © 2023 by KERRI COBY WHITE

All rights reserved. No part of this book may be reproduced or transmitted in any form or by any means without written permission from the author.

ISBN: 979-8-218-17328-9

Illustrations by Sheoli Chaturvedi

DISCLAIMER: The author makes no guarantees regarding results achieved by reading this book. All business requires risk. The results and client studies presented in this book represent results achieved working directly with the author and team. Results may vary.

CONTENTS

PART THREE: HOW TO BUILD YOUR MACHINE

FOREWORD

BY JAMES BROOKS

"Let's target the legal industry!"
"They have deep pockets!"
"We can make more in legal!"

This is how many vendors view law firms looking to grow their practice. Yours is an industry rich with experts and agencies preying on your success. Amidst a host of industry challenges, they know you need solutions for acquiring clients. They know you will pay for it, and they are only too willing to oblige and charge you accordingly.

The problem is, while some deliver in the short-term, most fail to deliver the long-term, sustainable growth you need.

Knowing this to be true, it gives me great pride to write this foreword and say a few words about Kerri Coby White.

My first encounter with Kerri was in 2018. She was an outlier in an online marketing forum for her incessant questioning of digital marketing outcomes. We continued the conversation offline and within six short months, agreed to partner.

With a background in both the investment and marketing industries, having worked across the globe, I was tasked with bringing the data-driven mindset to KerriJames. Kerri, though, is the yin to my yang. She is the extrovert amongst us. A people's person who cares deeply about doing well in business, not only for the partnership, but for her staff, her family, and, especially, her clients. The honesty and integrity she brings to the table is second to none as her client testimonials attest.

Behind this caring, friendly exterior is a woman of great drive, intellect, and capability. When you work with her, she gives it to you straight. She's insistent that hiring another agency, whether it be for SEO, Google PPC, or Facebook et al., will not deliver you the long-term growth objectives your firm needs.

At least not until the fundamentals for growth are first put in place.

It's a message she is passionate about. Those who have met her at events, heard her speak on stage, and/or listened to her on podcasts know this only too well. Amidst the ongoing noise of vendors pitching you tactics, Kerri stands apart. Her approach is founded on the age-old principles of strategy and systemization.

It's quite something to see her work her magic with law firms. Like a great actor that becomes the character they are playing in the movie, Kerri becomes part of your team. She takes your success personally. She revels in it and so leaves no stone unturned.

I'm proud to call her my business partner and am excited for the book you are about to read. It has the power to change the trajectory of your firm's growth if you take action.

Should you get the chance to work with her, grab it with both hands.

INTRODUCTION

Raise your hand if you picked up an MBA on your way to that JD. Exactly. Not many. If you've picked up this book, it's likely that you are as interested in growing your business and enjoying the success of your hard-earned (and expensive) degrees as you are practicing the law - the success you felt was firmly within your reach as an attorney.

Yet, for a shocking number, that success remains elusive. Lawyers are struggling. Professionally. Personally. Emotionally. Financially.

They are reluctantly letting go of the dream they once had of running a successful law practice, selling out to mega firms in some cases, swapping autonomy for stability, and relinquishing potential for predictable.

That's why I have written this book.

My partner James and I have spent decades around attorneys and in their businesses. We have seen the toll this inherently conflict-ridden industry has had on lawyers as it has become increasingly challenging and competitive. We have seen costs rise as predatory vendors seek to exploit what was once a profit-rich industry. We have watched eager-to-achieve attorneys "race to the top" in online bidding wars, shrinking margins dramatically as competition accelerates

We have experienced first-hand the stress and strain that comes with running a business without adequate business training.

Further, and quite alarmingly, online searches for terms like "lawyer anxiety," "lawyer depression," and even "lawyer suicide" are increasing at unprecedented rates. The industry - a necessary and noble one - is in crisis.

Our goal is to provide you with the very information and tools you need to grow a practice that is predictable, profitable, and growing. One that you find satisfying both as an attorney and as an entrepreneur and that allows you to enjoy financial success, peace of mind, and confidence that you have a thriving business while pursuing a passion for justice.

In the pages of this book, we will give you more than the concepts of our winning strategy and the systems that support it. We will give you the step-by-step method for building the system yourself. Further, we will avail ourselves to build it for you as we have for ourselves, for prestigious, enterprise-level firms, and for firms like yours, whether you are a solo practitioner or a multi-location office.

As busy consultants with our own thriving practice, you may wonder why we are offering you this very valuable information, information that we have honed over the course of many lucrative custom engagements with a wide variety of firms over years.

The answer is simple.

We want to help.

The years spent earning a law degree (and paying handsomely for it) should indeed position you for success. But, business growth isn't something your education likely prepared you for, nor did it account for the pace at which business has moved and changed over the last three decades let alone the last three years.

Sure, your undergraduate degree may have included some business classes, or you've attended enough conferences to have a foundation for building your practice. But, the realities of doing it all - and doing it well - are incredibly difficult, particularly for those who have had the unique training of learning to think like a lawyer - a character known to be so exceedingly thorough - that the industry notes a particularly slow adoption process with regard to new technology and tactics.

Changing Times

The pace of change isn't slowing down. Rather, it is accelerating. We are living through the Fourth Industrial Revolution, yet another period marked by sweeping changes in how work is done, and no industry is exempt. Whereas lawyers may have once been considered slow adopters, a new generation of attorneys stand ready to accept the challenge before them.

Opportunity will be limited to those prepared to operate and compete in this new world.

You can get your practice to a better place. A place in which you sign more clients, provide them the professional service you have proudly honed, increase revenue, drive down costs, and enjoy more time, financial freedom, and confidence that your practice, like your reputation, is consistently growing.

We want you to feel good about the important work you have chosen to do. Work that needs to be done!

There are no magic bullets. Online salesmen offering quick solutions can seldom bring results to bear in the long-term because they often offer *tactics* instead of *strategies* for growing your practice, but tactics change. Markets shift. Technology moves. Even people change.

Conversely, a commitment to a proven *strategy* supported by a robust *system* will future-proof your firm as tactics change, regardless of market shifts or new technologies. What we can provide you is tested and true and yours for the taking.

We call our solution The Law Firm Growth Machine.

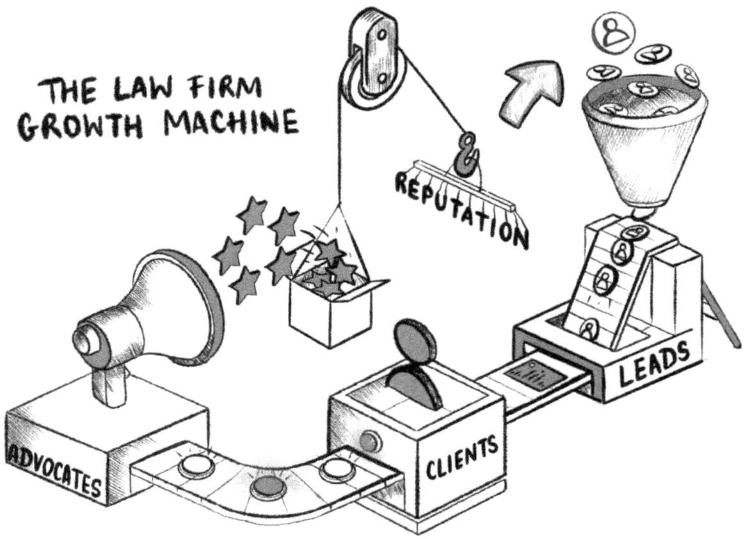

Here are the options we want to present to you:

1. You can use the information in this book to build a growth machine for your practice.

2. You can plug into the machine we've built after years of custom engagements, and within 30 days, set your practice on a course for success that is not only imminent but sustainable.

3. Or you can hire our team to build a machine to the very specific needs of your firm as we work closely with you to achieve the holy grail of growth: the flywheel effect.

Should you decide to proceed, you will set in place a plan to grow your business while enjoying the practice of law and building the life you planned.

About this Book

The book is broken into three distinct parts, and James, the function to my fashion, structure to my professional style, has expertly framed what I will cover in each. His brief introductions will guide us on this journey together so that you are prepared to extract from each segment the maximum value and knowledge required to transform your practice.

In Part 1, we will help you conceptualize a growth machine and provide context for why you need one. We'll introduce attorneys who have implemented a growth machine in their practice and evaluate the impact doing so has had on their lives.

You'll assess your firm's current condition and aptitude for change. We will reckon with the realities you must acknowledge if you endeavor to compete and win in this climate, and we will make the case to shift from the typical "treadmill" model you are likely on to one in which your business is fueling future growth with every client interaction.

In Part 2, we'll give you the winning strategy that has enabled us to help our clients achieve their practice goals of generating more opportunities, signing more clients, and turning those clients into powerful advocates that have tipped the scales of exponential growth for their practice. We'll also provide you with the very framework we utilize for systemizing that strategy so that you know precisely what your firm needs to do to grow with purpose and predictability.

We'll help set aside your lawyer hat to adopt the CEO's mentality necessary for competing in today's challenging environment as we address the fundamentals necessary for growing a profitable law practice.

Finally, in Part 3, we'll share the detailed steps, workflows, and even campaign language we've built into the systems that have helped our clients fuel their growth and design a practice they love.

Here's what's most exciting. At this very moment, you are standing on the precipice of profound change in your business. Our hope is that you will seize this opportunity to put this knowledge to work, or better yet, have our team do it for you.

If it sounds like a lot, let's break it down to the most simple components that we want you to internalize as we take on this material together:

1. You need a growth machine - a strategy and systems for growing your practice. Don't worry - we're going to give you both and explain why now is the time.

2. Your machine must employ proven tactics that capture leads, convert clients, and enhance your reputation. We tell you what you need to do to make that happen.

3. You need to grow like a CEO, adopting a business-minded, data-driven approach to growth, so that you can build and optimize your machine, identify opportunities, and sleep better at night. We show you how.

While we will give you the solution we've implemented for firms to accelerate growth in just 30 days, there are no shortcuts for sustaining this growth. It requires a daily commitment to numbers 1-3 above. Implement slowly or quickly, but note that success comes from a commitment to the solution at hand. There are no quick fixes.

Anyone who tells you otherwise is selling a tactic, and, again, tactics change.

Our team is here to help if you want to expedite that journey and plug into The Law Firm Growth Machine, our turnkey solution that has been tested in firms of all types and all sizes all across the country. If you want to build your own machine from scratch alongside our team but just want some help getting started, you're in the right place. If you want to plug into our machine, you can get started today. If you are looking to build a custom solution, like we have for clients from coast to coast, we're ready for you.

Wherever you are, just start the conversation with us, and know that the world can look very different in a very short matter of time. It doesn't have to be a struggle.

You have all the degrees you need. Now, you just need a proven way to turn that expertise into a thriving and satisfying business. I'd love to talk through your options on a strategy call soon!

Good luck! Let us know if we can help!

Kerri Coby White

Co-Founder | CEO, KerriJames

PART ONE

Why You Need a Growth Machine

A WORD FROM JAMES

A machine is a device or system that uses energy and/or power to perform a specific task or series of tasks, some more efficiently than others. Its goal, whether the machine is very complex or very simple (such as a hammer as compared to a coffee grinder), is to make work easier.

Now, imagine that you could use a machine to grow your law firm in an energy-efficient and highly effective manner. That's exactly what The Law Firm Growth Machine is designed to do.

In Part 1 of this book, Kerri's goal is to help you conceptualize The Law Firm Growth Machine and provide context for why now, more than ever, you need a growth machine for your law firm. Kerri walks you through a series of "Whys" so you can decide for yourself if you are ready to move forward.

The legal industry is facing challenges like never before. With technology disrupting traditional business models and changing client expectations, law firms need to adapt to stay competitive. Kerri explains in great detail why building a growth machine can help your law firm survive and thrive despite the mounting challenges and coming changes.

You may be wondering, what about small law firms and solo practitioners? Can they really compete with larger law firms?

Kerri says yes, and she should know.

Having traditionally worked with larger firms, she's codified what she's learned and adapted strategies and tactics to help smaller firms compete with those larger counterparts, and it's working for these small firms. Kerri introduces you to some of these clients who have committed to building and operating a growth machine in their practice. Though their names have been changed to protect their privacy and competitive edge, their stories and the challenges they faced are authentic. They've gained greater control over their practice and business growth and gained a renewed passion for the practice of law as a result.

Of course, growth isn't easy. There are some harsh realities that law firms must accept if they want to move forward. Kerri gives these to you straight. It might be a little uncomfortable at times to admit to some of these realities, but tackling these challenges head-on will serve you well in your pursuit of long-term, sustainable growth. In fact, by failing to accept them, I'd suggest you're setting yourself up for failure.

As Kerri alluded to in the Introduction, one of the cornerstones of sustainable growth is having the right systems in place. She explains why systems are so important and why failing to systemize will lead to problems further down the line, but she also cautions against building systems without a solid strategy. Without a clear plan in place, even the best systems will fail.

So, let's get started and set the foundations in Part 1. Once you understand the why, you'll be better positioned for the practical advice to come in later parts of this book.

"

The best way to predict your future is to create it.

ABRAHAM LINCOLN

CHAPTER 1

BEGIN WITH THE END IN MIND

Imagine for a moment that, instead of reading this book, you were featured as a case study after successfully implementing The Law Growth Machine in your practice.

I'd be writing of your growing business, utter control over your practice, reinvestment in your passions, and optimism for the future.

That's exactly what our clients report and what we want for you too.

James and I have been working together for about five years now. When we met, I'd been serving attorneys in a business development capacity for over a decade. My focus on interpersonal strategies helped law firms build a loyal client base, cultivate referral partnerships, and develop new business.

Meanwhile, as a former investment analyst, James was skilled in analysis and obsessed with data. Surrounded by a family of lawyers, after years in the financial industry, he started to work with law firms on their data-driven approaches to marketing and growth.

A modern practice required what James and I could better deliver collectively - an approach to growth that marries the personal and digital, the empathetic and automatic, especially as social media resulted in a true consumers' economy.

Our message resonated with attorneys, primarily from large firms with significant resources, who understood that neither analog nor digital marketing alone would suffice in an increasingly challenging landscape, and before long, we had signed clients who were as interested in our growth strategy and lead-generating tactics as our brand design and intake consulting. They valued the tools we implemented to optimize for the strategy and adopted a business mindset (tracking, measuring, investing) that drove success across collaborative teams.

We cut our teeth with some of the most complex intake departments handling leads generated by 7-figure marketing budgets.

We often found that we brought order to chaos, surprised that some of these huge practices in shiny buildings over gleaming cities were actually lacking the underpinnings that could make them not just huge but hugely successful.

It was humbling to find that those shiny exteriors didn't always reflect what was happening in those inner offices.

Over the years, we have adapted our strategy, codifying the lessons of our high-end consulting engagements to meet the needs of solo, small, and mid-sized practices at can't-afford-not-to pricing. In so doing, we have had the opportunity to work alongside hard-working, growth-minded, and justice-seeking attorneys to transform underperforming practices into client-generating machines in which several outcomes were realized:

- First and foremost, we built confidence in our clients that they could achieve their goals in their practice. For some, it was about generating 7-figures per month. For others, it was about spending time serving clients. And others - well, one - who didn't want to interrupt his morning workouts on the beach. We gave each of them the keys to achieving that success and, thus, the peace of mind that comes with such control.

- We watched as attorneys fell in love with their practice - some for the first time. Our clients were excited by the opportunities in front of them, relishing a renewed passion for the actual practice of law, enjoying the responsibility and pride that comes with employing others, and the satisfaction of growing influence in their respective communities.

- We were able to identify where the best leads were coming from, the cost to get them there, and the return on investment, laying the foundation for growth that opened the door to new and exciting opportunities.

- We all but eliminated intake overwhelm on teams who expressed a newfound calm and control that enabled them to engage more empathetically with their callers, follow up in meaningful ways, and build rapport that resulted in positive feedback and improved company culture.

- We improved the online reputation for our clients, which increases attention and general inquiries and aids in conversion, resulting in an overall decrease in the cost to acquire a new client.

- We created systems that enabled practices to better serve prospects and clients, leading to better client experiences, referral business, further reputation enhancement, and genuine fans of the practice who act as firm advocates.

In short, what we accomplished with each engagement was a shift in how business was generated. We dismantled the traditional funnel and created a *flywheel effect* for our clients, an approach to growth in which strategic investments in the business generate results that compound over time, building nearly unstoppable momentum.

Momentum.

Let's study that word for a moment. Merriam-Webster defines momentum as "strength or force gained by motion or by a series of events."

The irony here is in the phrase "series of events," which is completely contrary to the first six letters of the word: *moment*.

Moment suggests a singular point in time. An ah-ha *moment*; the right *moment*, having a *moment*. That's exactly what growth and the flywheel effect is **NOT** about. It's not about a singular moment or act. It's lots of moments, delivered consistently over time, compounding and building the momentum that transforms a business' trajectory.

What we have provided for our clients, and what we can deliver for you, is not a single event or tactic but a defined strategy, a system for implementing that strategy, and a closed loop to constantly improve that system and accelerate growth.

It's a growth machine that makes it possible to achieve the flywheel effect.

If you aren't familiar with the flywheel effect, don't worry. We're going to dive deeper into the simplicity and effectiveness of the flywheel and introduce you to the strategy at the center of The Law Firm Growth Machine, a turnkey solution for developing new business that, when implemented and consistently executed, will transform your practice.

But first, let's look at a few examples of what we've achieved with our clients and what we can help you achieve in your practice by creating a system to set your flywheel in motion.

Take Scott, for example.

CASE STUDY #1: Solo Bankruptcy Attorney

- Unpredictable business
- Unable to step away from the practice
- Lacking confidence in where to invest
- Working without realizing financial benefits

Scott, a dedicated bankruptcy attorney in a large metropolitan market, was living (as he described it) hand to mouth. The only business he generated came from referrals and those he knew personally, and those calls were coming less frequently.

His website was completely buried on Google and did nothing to attract or convert cases. Though his clients adored him, he wasn't generating new business with any regularity. He was insecure about the next client to come through the door and chronically facing the strain of school tuition payments and childcare costs.

Scott was incredibly frustrated. He knew he provided clients with a game-changing solution to their problems and was skilled at what he did, but he didn't know how to generate new cases. He lived glued to his cell phone, always worried the next call might be a "good case." Even so, Scott frequently missed opportunities (not to mention wrestling matches and a few family dinners).

By first recognizing what Scott did best (outstanding service), we were able to define his growth strategy and set his flywheel in motion.

Leveraging Scott's existing client base, we ran a review request campaign in which Scott quickly generated a healthy number of enthusiastic, five-star, online reviews, immediately elevating his online presence and re-engaging his client base.

We built a system for responding to missed calls, buying Scott a little time when he needed it, and outsourced specific campaign calls altogether, allowing only qualified prospects to make it to Scott's hands. This solution also enabled Scott to step away from his phone when he needed to be focused on other tasks - including personal ones.

We connected Scott with trusted partners in the industry to build a cost-effective website that was optimized for lead capture and conversion, integrating directly with his intake system. We invested in lead generation with robust tracking to ensure we could identify the highest quality lead sources, and we relentlessly tracked conversion to ensure positive ROI and strategic reinvestment moving forward.

We built a robust follow-up system utilizing automation to ensure that every possible conversion was captured without absorbing valuable time.

We implemented a review request campaign on the backside of new client intake that ensured every contact was given the opportunity to provide feedback regarding their experience and that positive feedback was shared publicly.

In time, Scott's online presence in a huge city was impressive. His clients raved about the dedicated care and concern he provided, the helpful nature with which he approached even callers he *couldn't* help, and the trust they had in his ability to resolve their problems.

One year later, Scott is confidently employing two others, enjoying time away from his business, and driving down his client acquisition costs. He effectively plans for new business based on his marketing investments and is grateful to be paying tuition on time every month.

Scott's practice is positioned for long-term, sustainable growth, and he is excited for the future.

CASE STUDY #2: Large, multi-state personal injury practice

- High acquisition costs
- Inconsistent ROI
- Overwhelmed intake staff
- Poor reviews

The John P. Firm is an established practice with a large team and brand recognition. Firm leadership was perplexed by their relatively poor performance and escalating costs after years of successfully growing their practice. During our initial consultation, we found, like many of the firms we work with, they were unable to answer some fundamental questions about the practice:

- What is your average cost of acquisition?
- Where are your best leads coming from?
- What's the average case value?

Despite a very generous monthly budget, the firm was not generating the results they anticipated and sought to reach their goals which included maintaining a large staff, office real estate, and case investments to which they were committed.

The intake team was chasing leads but lacked a consistent follow-up system. Leads were entered in spreadsheets, delivered to inboxes, passed out on pink slips, and occasionally, missed entirely.

Online reviews suggested calls were ignored, staff was rude, and general service was poor. Leadership was concerned by escalating costs, staff turnover, and a diminishing reputation.

To fuel growth, we had to, first and foremost, determine where the best cases were coming from and fund those sources adequately. Robust tracking and reporting were critical.

The team needed efficiency tools that provided thorough follow-up campaigns and allowed them the time to connect personally with clients and prospects, responding empathetically to the callers' needs.

With happier callers, we needed to leverage a review request at precisely the right time to remediate online review scores.

Within months, we were able to identify the best lead sources and the cost of acquisition. The intake team reported a sense of control over the lead flow and the ability to more effectively convert callers. Referral business increased. We confidently invested in the best lead channels, continued to generate positive reviews, and drove growth while squeezing even more out of the already generous budget.

CASE STUDY #3: Referral Practice Partnership

Ben and Mike figured out some time ago that they had distinctly different skills within their partnership that they respectively enjoyed and at which they excelled.

Ben was great at marketing, generating new business at good prices, and spending time with his Pomeranians. Mike was great at converting leads into clients and getting in a sweat-inducing beach workout before noon.

What they didn't love was the actual work of settling personal injury claims with insurance companies. In fact, the two became so effective at their individual roles that they found, financially, the benefit of doing the work themselves wasn't worth the additional earnings they could generate as compared to setting up a referral practice.

For years, the practice had been operating as co-counsel to firms with whom they had partnerships. But, as internet pricing escalated, competition increased, and frankly, tides rose on those beachfront workouts. Ben and Mike were ready to create even more of a lifestyle practice.

The work of retaining clients, tracking referral agreements, and following up on case statuses was time-consuming. Identifying the best lead sources was challenging, and as prices increased, Ben realized he needed to leverage their reputation and ensure that every possible lead was converted.

We implemented The Law Firm Growth Machine for the team that delivered leads to Mike's cell phone - even while on the beach. From an app, he was able to simply "drag and drop" to automate the delivery of a retainer and notify referral partners of new clients. A follow-up system encouraged prospects to take action while status update requests saved Mike from countless manual emails chasing their shared clients. Again, review request campaigns ensured that the partners' online reputation was augmented, helping to further attract business and drive acquisition costs down.

Today, Ben and Mike have a true lifestyle practice. They enjoy transparency in the success of their marketing efforts, have eliminated most manual tasks that kept them in front of their computers, and regained a tremendous amount of time while spending less to earn more.

The Ingredients to Succeed

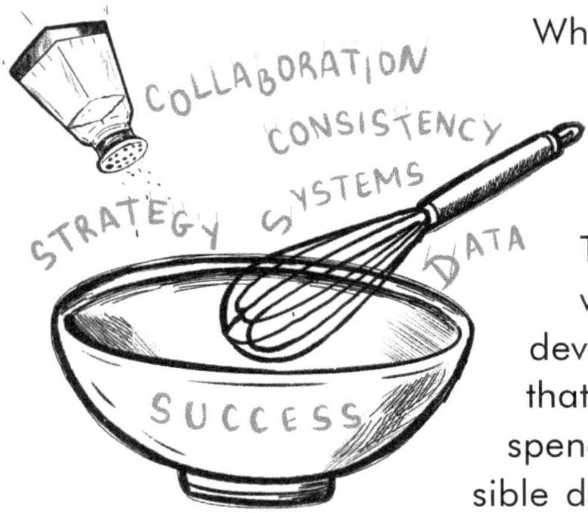

What have all these clients achieved that you, too, can achieve in your practice?

They have honed in on what they do well and devised a strategy around that. To enable them to spend as much time as possible doing what they do best, they have built systems that execute the strategy with efficiency and consistency. They let the system inform their decision-making so that they can invest strategically in growth. Their efforts compound over time because of their commitment to the strategy and oversight of the system, generating the flywheel effect in their business.

To further simplify, our clients:

1. Systemized their strategy to save time and deliver results with consistency
2. Broke down silos and aligned teams to achieve their growth goals
3. Tracked and leveraged data to make more informed and profitable decisions
4. Committed to their systems and, ultimately, their long-term success

Our clients are thriving and growing despite a challenging space in a quickly changing environment. They are no longer anxious about making payroll, taking vacation time with their families, or questioning their ability to maintain their own practices instead of selling out to become a salaried employee in some other firm. They are seeing the benefits of having invested in their education and are building not only the practice they imagined - but the life they imagined too.

In the chapters that follow, we will explain exactly how these clients went from anxious and overwhelmed to in control and enthusiastic and how you can start that same transformation in the next 30 days - or even less.

But hear this: The Law Firm Growth Machine isn't a quick fix - it's a committed fix. As I've warned, there are no quick fixes. Any consultant or marketer who tells you otherwise is selling false hope in the form of tactics that may offer short-term wins but will fail to deliver long-term results. In the same way a fad diet ultimately leads to weight gain, quick fixes in your business will have similarly untenable results if you fail to make lasting changes to how you operate. Conversely, over the next 30 days or even less, you can take actions that will set the flywheel in motion, positioning your firm for success tomorrow and well beyond.

I'll leave you with this analogy. Growth is a lot like organization. Getting organized is nothing compared to staying organized. On a rainy Sunday, you can take your pantry and alphabetize the canned goods. But, when you rush home from the market on a busy Tuesday night, will you have the commitment to place the black beans ahead of the garbanzo beans?

Growing your practice isn't a one-time fix. It's a commitment that not all attorneys can make. It's why we built our machine to streamline growth while providing attorneys with the insights they need to make data-driven growth decisions.

"

Strength does not come from physical capacity. It comes from an indomitable will.

MAHATMA GANDHI

CHAPTER 2

WHO THIS BOOK IS FOR

Stress in the legal space isn't new. Lawyering in and of itself is a stressful job without the complications of running a profitable business in a challenging environment, and it's really no wonder.

No one contacts a law office because they are excitedly planning a summer vacation. Prospects contact lawyers because they're facing a conflict or crisis: a collision, a divorce, having been charged with a crime, suffering a personal injury, etc. As conflict resolvers, first-responders really, attorneys are programmed to take on someone else's burdens when things go wrong. That alone is stressful.

The internal expectations can be equally debilitating.

Many lawyers have extremely high expectations of themselves, attributes baked into the attorney persona after years of cutthroat competition getting into the right undergrad program, the right law school, or the right clerkships.

When things don't pan out the way one may have hoped, these same individuals are particularly hard on themselves, even to the detriment of pivoting to improve a poor situation. What results is a corps of very high-achieving people living in a world of conflict. Partners, in particular, have the added stress and strain of keeping a team employed. They worry that they will let down the people who work for them if their ability to attract new business dries up.

Obviously, clients are the lifeblood of a practice. Yet, in an incredibly competitive space, attracting new business is difficult. Today, 72% of law firms state it's a challenge to acquire clients[1]. While most attorneys would prefer their business

---

1 https://www.thomsonreuters.com/en-us/posts/wp-content/uploads/sites/20/022/11/State-of-Small-Law-Firms-2022.pdf

come from "word-of-mouth," 96% of consumers begin their search for an attorney online[2]. Practices must therefore invest time and effort into online marketing. But again, due to the competitive nature of the industry, doing so is expensive and requires skills that are not necessarily present in every law firm (digital marketing wasn't on the JD curriculum either).

Although a vast network of "experts" offer these services, it's difficult to tell who's good and who's seeking to profit off an industry with historically significant margins. Given that the most expensive legal term keyword can top four figures, such "investments" can prove particularly costly if those clicks don't become clients.

All these factors - competition, expense, expectations - have taken their toll.

Only 50% of lawyers are satisfied with their work-life balance. The suicide rate is horrifyingly high among attorneys. Twenty-one percent of lawyers admit to having a drinking problem according to a widely circulated study by the American Bar Association and Hazelden Betty Ford Center, and the rate of addiction among attorneys is said to be two to three and a half times greater than in other professions[3].

At the risk of sounding like a 1980s infomercial, I'm going to say what you may be thinking:

There has to be a better way!

Thankfully, there is, and we're going to reveal it throughout the balance of this book.

----

2 https://www.nivancontent.com/law-firm-marketing-statistics-2019/

3 https://www.americanbar.org/groups/senior_lawyers/publications/voice_of_experience/2021/voice-of-experience-november-2021/dissenting-from-death-preventing-lawyer-suicide/

Understanding the Struggle

Having worked in business development in the legal industry for over a decade, and having endured the painful lessons of growing our own business, James and I came to understand the stress and strain that attorneys experience in growing their firms all too well.

As noted, attorneys expect an awful lot of themselves. That often means they expect a lot of others too - especially those they trust in deploying resources and chasing growth. Like attorneys practicing in such a competitive space, making decisions about strategic investments like James and I do isn't exactly a cakewalk in the current climate. For folks like us, particularly James in his former role as an investment analyst, and myself, the uber-empath, the emotional roller coaster that comes with putting other people's hard-earned money to work in such a challenging environment is all too familiar.

Regretfully, we've learned over the years that our obsessive determination to win for our clients wasn't near as universal as we would have expected.

Frankly, there are too many marketing firms who consider their work done at the click.

**But firms aren't paying for clicks.
They are paying for clients.**

What has made us unique as a growth partner is what so many "tactitioners" (you'll learn more about tactics in the pages to come) fail to recognize:

Growth is seldom attributed to any one thing.

Marketing (strategic marketing, that is) can be a direct line to growth, but sadly, again clicks aren't clients and few agencies follow through from click to client. Boasting impressive impression share, site visitors or clicks isn't sufficient. Vanity metrics don't pay the bills and increasing lead volume can actually result in lower conversions and higher acquisition costs.

Moving Beyond Vanity Metrics

These lessons came into sharp focus during an engagement we had with a large personal injury firm that enjoyed brand recognition and a sizable budget. They hired us after letting go of their marketing agency when increasing budgets failed to move the needle in their business.

A deep dive into the firm's intake, client service, and reputation revealed significant gaps not only in operations but in strategy that, left unaddressed, would undermine any marketing team's efforts.

James and I set out to solve these problems as so many problems today are solved - with technology. We streamlined their intake pipeline, then implemented follow-up campaigns and communication tools. We installed robust tracking and automation so that the team could spend time on tasks that required human interaction, not tasks that could be left to machines.

More importantly, we defined a strategy and built systems to support it.

Our strategy and the system we built to execute it was the result of the unique strengths James and I each brought to the table and a winning combination for our clients.

Why?

Because we solved the problems that so many attorneys were facing given the current climate that very much aligned with who they wanted to be professionally and personally.

- Our attorneys value great legal work as well as client service and endeavor to be a client-centered firm.
- They believe their staff needs to operate with empathy and compassion despite the many demands on their time.
- They relish a stellar reputation and want to be known and respected in their community.
- They believe that the right technology can solve some of the challenges they face.
- They are willing to invest in marketing so long as they can track the outcomes and realize a positive return on this investment.
- They recognize the importance of systemizing lead capture and conversion as a way to improve conversion rates and drive down acquisition costs.
- They accept the increased competition and general challenges but recognize a steadfast commitment to their strategy and systems as a means to address them.
- They understand the importance of operating as a CEO - they are data-driven, collaborative, and focused on building a successful business.

If you recognize yourself or your firm in anything you've read, let me assure you that you are not alone. The difficulties law firms face are well documented, and the way in which

business has changed in the age of the internet (not to mention how it will only change further in "The Fourth Industrial Revolution") has made for a turbulent period.

Let's quickly address what is meant by "The Fourth Industrial Revolution."

We are living in a wild moment of transformation. The use of machine learning, artificial intelligence, and data analytics (in just the last year!) is transforming how people connect and communicate and how businesses grow. Failure to adopt shifting strategies and tactics will significantly affect a firm's ability to compete with those who do. Given recent changes to allowable business structures (who can claim an ownership stake in a practice), this is an incredibly important reckoning.

The legal industry is considered to be a particularly slow-moving space. In fact, in December of 2018, exactly one year before the genesis of COVID-19, Forbes magazine presciently declared, "The Legal Industry Is Not Prepared For Digital Consumers." The piece continued, "The legal industry's overall lack of digital awareness and preparedness is a serious problem that is seldom discussed."[4]

What's especially encouraging, though, and as COVID proved, is that the legal industry typically outperforms other

---

4 https://www.forbes.com/sites/markcohen1/2018/12/20/law-is-lagging-digital-transformation-why-it-matters/?sh=26226536515c

industries when facing economic crises. As Alton Weil put it in their annual report "Law Firms in Transition," (first published in the aftermath of The Great Recession) attorneys seem to have a particular penchant for proving they can do hard things - when pushed to do so. The pandemic certainly pushed many firms to make digital progress in how they attract clients, deliver service, and operate their business.[5]

Further, as the Boomers prepare to retire (after several economically-driven delays) the newest partners moving into firm leadership are Digital Natives.

Say Hello to Your New Partners

Digital Natives, those born and raised during the digital age, are entering leadership positions and bringing with them their comfort and expertise in technology and digital media. This shift is leading to a new approach to business with a focus on innovation and efficient use of technology.

Digital Natives are known for their multitasking skills and ability to quickly adapt to new technologies, making them well-suited to lead companies through the rapidly changing digital landscape. These skills could prove especially important as economic indicators suggest greater challenges on the horizon.

5 https://altmanweil.com/wp-content/uploads/2022/06/Law-Firms-in-Transition-2020-An-Altman-Weil-Flash-Survey-.pdf

As the Digital Natives take on leadership roles throughout the industry, businesses can expect to see a greater emphasis on data-driven decision making, increased use of automation, and a focus on digital transformation initiatives. All of these adjustments will be necessary to address in a modern firm, especially in light of new business models for delivering legal services and the shift in partnership structures enabling non-attorneys to have equity stakes in firms. This means that in addition to competing with attorneys, you can expect to compete with partner-level financial, technology and marketing professionals.

So, congratulations!

You are reading this book and are ready to make a change in how you grow your business.

After years of very high-end consulting engagements, we have codified those experiences to build The Law Firm Growth Machine. We are ready to divulge the ways in which our clients put their practice into overdrive and began to function in a way that addresses the challenges they face and seizes the opportunity at hand. It is possible!

As a lawyer, you solve a problem that only specialized providers can solve. That comes at a premium to potential clients. The average attorney invoice is a substantial figure. Every single client has significant value to your practice, and solving for some of the small challenges that prevent your team from generating leads and turning those leads into clients will profoundly impact your aptitude for growth. Employing a strategy and implementing a system around that strategy will bear fruit when you commit to ruthless

execution and adherence and have the tools you need to stay the course.

You. Can. Do. This.

The Law Firm Growth Machine is a proven solution and is one you can plug into even before you finish this book if you so choose. Take these pages and run with our recommendations or hire our team to work with you to make your dream practice a reality!

Closing Arguments

- Lawyering is an innately noble, necessary, but stressful job with high expectations and cutthroat competition. Attracting new clients is challenging in an extremely competitive industry. The challenges have taken a toll, but there is a better way! We're sharing that way with you in these pages.

- The legal industry has outperformed other industries during hard times and is poised to do so in The Fourth Industrial Revolution if attorneys act now and take action. As Boomers retire, Digital Natives are entering leadership positions and bringing with them their comfort and expertise in technology, leading to a focus on innovation, efficient use of technology, data-driven decision-making, increased automation, and digital transformation initiatives, all of which will be necessary in addressing new business models in the industry.

- Employing a strategy and building a system around that strategy can profoundly impact a law firm's aptitude for growth by ensuring ruthless adherence to both. After years of high-end consulting engagements, James and I created The Law Firm Growth Machine, a turnkey solution that any law firm, of any size, can either recreate or plug into. We will share how you can do this for your firm.

Self Assessment

Let's take inventory before we go any further and assess where your practice is at present:

For each of the statements below, rate yourself on a scale from 1 - 5 on how accurate the statements are—1 means "not accurate at all," and 5 means "most accurate."

Next, total up your score and use the Answer Key to determine your next steps.

- ☐ I can confidently invest in my business and anticipate the return on investment
- ☐ I can identify my firm's greatest strengths.
- ☐ I know where most of our business comes from.
- ☐ I am informed and, thus, make sound decisions about my business instead of reacting or making gut decisions.
- ☐ My reputation is always improving online.
- ☐ We never miss phone calls at my practice.
- ☐ I can plan for the future without fear of business drying up.
- ☐ I know how many prospective client calls I generate per month.
- ☐ I know the percentage of my prospective client calls that convert to clients.

- ☐ I know the cost per acquisition for each of my lead sources.
- ☐ I know which lead source results in the highest quality cases.
- ☐ I never worry about making payroll.
- ☐ I never worry about someone on the team resigning.
- ☐ I can take a vacation and my business still thrives.
- ☐ I'm a good partner, spouse, and parent - low on stress and high on energy.
- ☐ I don't suffer the emotional strain of many of my legal industry colleagues - depression, anxiety, or substance abuse.
- ☐ My firm is client-centered and values high quality service.
- ☐ I recognize the importance and value of my reputation online and off.
- ☐ I use technology to solve some of the challenges the industry currently faces.
- ☐ I invest in new business and can determine the return on investment.
- ☐ We have a strategy we are committed to and systems around that strategy ensure we operate in alignment with the strategy.
- ☐ I am the CEO of my firm - data-driven, collaborctive, and growth-minded.

Answer key

22-49

Your score falls in the low range, indicating that you may struggle to grow your law practice effectively. Consider seeking out resources and tools that can help you better understand and manage your practice, such as legal marketing, business development, or client relationship management courses.

50-79

Your score falls in the moderate range, indicating that you have some strengths but also areas for improvement. Consider focusing on the statements where you scored lower, such as understanding your client acquisition costs or tracking the sources of your leads. Seek out additional support and resources to help you improve in those areas, and consider implementing new systems to improve your practice's efficiency and effectiveness.

80-110

Your score falls in the high range, indicating that you have strong skills and are well-positioned for growing a successful law practice. You may already have a good understanding of your business metrics and may be well-versed in legal marketing and client relationship management. Continue to build on your strengths and consider using your expertise to mentor others or take on new challenges to further expand your practice.

"

The truth will set you free, but first it will make you miserable.

JAMES A. GARFIELD

CHAPTER 3

THE HARSH REALITIES

I'm a chronic journaler, and as decades of my handwritten diaries stack up, I find I can identify some very clear, deeply-held beliefs about what it means to run a business and the kind of business I want to be recognized for running.

Some of my earliest musings as a business owner reflect a wide-eyed naïveté that I now recognize as an obstacle to scale and one that Jim Collins discusses in his book *Good to Great:*

The very nature of business is that as volume increases, quality typically declines.

Even Jerry Maguire himself tapped out in his impassioned mission statement: Fewer clients. Less money.

I'm certain that, for many passionate attorneys-at-law, the idea of serving fewer clients with a higher quality of service is intriguing as a model. It's a noble concept if you are content to make a humble income or your service is so superior that a premium pricing model can be employed (think A-list hair stylist, five-star dining, and high-end business consultants with costs that intentionally dissuade prospects from hiring them).

Unfortunately, in the legal services industry, this is increasingly difficult, particularly given the growth of the attorney population amidst a decline in demand. As Altman Weil wrote in 2018:

> *"The overall demand for legal services has decreased in the aggregate since the recession, and all of the dynamics that affect hours available to traditional law firms clearly indicate a continuing downward trend. Commoditization, new technology tools, and 'non-traditional' competitors are all permanent changes to a post-recession market. Demand for law firm services will not return to pre-recession levels – ever.*

Sure, there are some attorneys who have established so revered a reputation that they can bill exorbitant fees, but by and large, the space has become commoditized and saturated. For many, serving volume is necessary to keep the fires burning, the staff paid, and, for personal injury firms especially, opportunities for "the big one" on the horizon.

That's just one of the harsh realities in the space that we must work to address if you want to build a thriving practice and enjoy the fruits of your labor.

In our years working with attorneys, we've found plenty of other challenges that we routinely seek to address. These are often the obstacles inhibiting our clients' growth and preventing them from living the life they imagined as the successful founder of a respected law firm.

Look, I want to help, but I want to help the attorneys who are ready to win, to face the challenges, accept the realities, and commit to a proven approach. At risk of offending, I'm going to give it to you straight, because here's the truth: the industry is saturated. We don't need all these lawyers competing for the same client pool, especially as demand shrinks. So, if you don't want to deal with the harsh realities and seek to overcome them, then you might as well step aside for someone who will.

The industry is changing. An onslaught of funding from investors and new laws allowing non-lawyer partnerships in particular are priming the industry for significant disruption. Technology and artificial intelligence in particular are creating sweeping change across every industry. It's well advised to heed the words of Leon C. Megginson, a Louisiana State University business professor, who captured the essence of Charles Darwin in 1963 when he said, "It is not the strongest of the species that survives, nor the most intelligent, but the one most responsive to change."

Harsh Reality #1: You aren't keeping up.

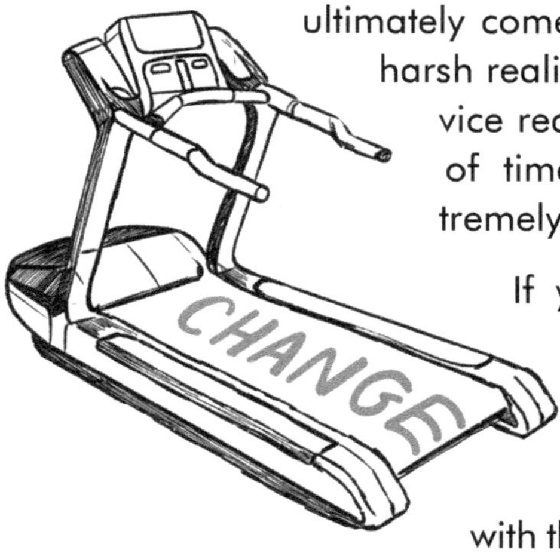

You are in a service-driven industry, so it will ultimately come down to service (that's a harsh reality in and of itself). But, service requires an extensive amount of time and energy that is extremely costly.

If you haven't adopted technology or begun to utilize data and AI in meaningful ways, it's unlikely you are able to keep up with the demands of service while managing your cases and running a practice (or compete with those who do). Identifying the right solutions, learning the systems, implementing, and continually improving are all a matter of slowing down to speed up, and many firms have failed to do so.

In the same 2018 report, Altman Weil wrote:

> *Without a crisis, it's hard to create a sense of urgency. But waiting for a crisis is never a good strategy, as then any actions you take will come too late.*[6]

But wait we did.

Many firms are still behind when it comes to adopting the technology that enables them to compete in this market.

---

6 https://altmanweil.com/wp-content/uploads/2022/06/Law-Firms-in-Transition-2018-An-Altman-Weil-Flash-Survey-.pdf

This is after COVID-19 presented just the crisis many firms needed to progress (and kudos to the many that did!)!

Can your clients text you?

Can they self-serve on your website?

Can they make digital payments or access their file online?

Can they message you on social media or through your Google Business Profile and receive a timely response?

If you've answered no, then you are not keeping up with consumer expectations or with your competitors.

Technology is the only way small firms have any chance of competing with large firms, and frankly, because they lack economies of scale, the cost of failing to slow down and implement the right technology is even greater for smaller firms.

Here's the good news.

With the Digital Natives stepping up, the days of blasting firms for lagging on their technology adoption are likely to end.

Given the current economic forecast, we anticipate those newly minted partners to make dramatic changes that will prove once again that attorneys are made of some pretty tough stuff.

The Law Firm Growth Machine leverages technology, AI, and data to help busy attorneys save time and energy so that you can practice law and empower your team to provide the kind of service that makes clients of leads and advocates of clients - things machines cannot do as well.

Harsh Reality #2: You can't do this alone.

Does your marketing team know exactly which leads resulted in signed cases? Does your intake team know who left that lousy online review? More importantly, do they know why? If you are working with outsourced teams, is communication between those service providers facilitated? Or, if you are working alone, are you connecting the dots between these various stages of the lead-to-client journey?

Operating in silos creates a false sense of achievement for each of the individuals or teams tasked with growing your firm. How we define success will vary wildly from team to team if we don't work beyond our respective roles within the firm.

The critical growth systems in your firm are Marketing, Intake, and Service.

Marketing will measure success by looking at ad performance, click-through rates, and online conversion metrics. Those are very important to measuring campaign performance, but in isolation, they do not grow a firm or pay the bills.

In intake, more leads *can* mean more opportunity, but it always means more screening time. If those leads aren't converting, then what is the value in that volume? Fewer high-quality leads increase the opportunity for conversion while high-volume, low-quality leads can overwhelm the team and actually inhibit growth. If intake and marketing aren't communicating, how is success measured?

Similarly, feedback from the team (or individual) managing reputation is essential for improving service delivery and conversions, and building brand awareness. Every review - good or bad - is an opportunity to improve. Increasingly, consumers take to social media and other online forums to criticize even a receptionist who responds a little too abruptly. This feedback is a gift to your firm if you choose to learn from it.

When good reviews come in, that information can not only be used to promote the firm (send it back to the marketing team!) but to develop your continuous training programs so that tactics resulting in happy clients and positive reviews can be replicated.

You can't do it alone. We are living in an ever-more highly specialized era, and it's okay that, despite your academic success and general aptitude, you don't have all the answers. If you invest in the right partners to grow your practice, or market your firm, or develop your technology, or train your team, and you facilitate the collaboration of their efforts, you will realize an impressive return on your investment.

The beauty of this moment is that you don't have to know it all. I'll never argue a case before a judge, and you'll likely never deliver a presentation about the power of an intelligence loop in driving growth. That's okay!

The Law Firm Growth Machine is a collaborative model, and you are the CEO overseeing its successful execution.

Harsh Reality #3: You don't know your numbers.

As growth consultants, we incorporate data into every decision. In recent decades, the companies that have achieved unprecedented growth haven't done so by chance - they have done so by making decisions based on the intelligence their data conveys.

At a minimum, you must be able to report the following:

What is the average value of a case to your firm?

Many personal injury attorneys in particular get uncomfortable with this question, but it is imperative to any firm seeking success. If it makes you more comfortable to ignore the top and bottom 10%, then do so, but if you intend to practice for many years, these "outliers" are part of the equation that must be accounted for! Due to market saturation, personal injury attorneys are operating largely at modest returns while awaiting the "big one." They come to those patient enough to participate in the game.

What are your campaign conversion rates?

It's important that conversion is assessed by campaign. Various campaigns have various costs that need to be accounted for when assessing the success of an initiative. If you have a high-volume campaign that only converts at 5%, then is it worth busying your team with those calls? Would it be worthwhile to outsource those calls? These are decisions that can only be made when you know your numbers.

What is your average acquisition cost?

Again, campaign-level metrics will be incredibly important, but overall, you need to know how much you are spending and what you are achieving, especially since most leads will interact with your brand across multiple channels before taking action. At the campaign level, you can optimize for the highest conversion rates or best leads, but generally, you need to know what you are spending and what it is generating in return. Only then can you make decisions that improve your outcomes while maintaining a diverse marketing portfolio to safeguard your growth.

What is your ROI?

Marketing done well is an investment, not an expense. Therefore, the calculation you need to make to grow your firm is simply one of Return on Investment. Growth-minded attorneys must look to increase ROI. To do so, you need to either reduce the cost of acquiring a new client and/or increase the value of each new client you bring on.

Attorneys with a firm grasp of their numbers are able to make capital allocation and operational decisions that drive growth. Basic reporting built into The Law Firm Growth Machine will put this information at your fingertips. Key Performance Indicators (KPIs) will empower your team, improve your decision-making, and supercharge your growth.

Harsh Reality #4: It's Google's world. We're just living in it.

The company, so ubiquitous it became a verb, wields tremendous power over our ability to generate business. Those of us that fight that truth will find ourselves in a losing battle.

Appeasing the Google gods means that you accept that the days of a client sending you a strongly worded letter or email expressing disappointment are long gone. Instead, that disgruntled client is taking to Google to leave a scathing review for all the world - including prospective clients - to see.

If we ignore the demands of Google - the company controlling "near me" searches and maps - we will struggle to compete.

The growth machine we're going to help you build centralizes communications from a multitude of platforms including Google, and facilitates soliciting feedback. This feeds Google's algorithm with tasty delights that build your firm's online presence and make Google more likely to present your services as consumers' solution.

Your growth machine will also push those glowing reviews to the community through your social channels, increasing awareness of your firm and elevating your reputation in a social-proof-driven era.

Harsh Reality #5: Your competition is increasing.

If it feels like there are more lawyers than ever, it's not just your network. The legal industry in the United States is growing at an astonishing rate, with the number of lawyers increasing exponentially over the past century.

In fact, the number of attorneys in the U.S. grew 793% between 1900 and 2000, exceeding the growth of the population. This growth has been particularly rapid in recent decades, with the number of lawyers doubling between 1950 and 1978 alone! If you are a lawyer operating in a large, metro area, you may find yourself facing even greater competition, with as many as 14 lawyers per 1,000 residents.[7]

Industry surveys routinely report that the greatest challenge lawyers face is acquiring new clients. An increase in the number of lawyers, diluted prospect pools resulting from decentralized media, mega-firms squeezing out smaller practices, and escalating costs are but a few of the reasons it's just gotten harder to get work.

This is all happening amidst a decline in demand for traditional legal services and the birth of alternative legal service providers. These providers offer more affordable and flexible options for clients, including online legal services and legal process outsourcing. The growth of technology and globalization has also contributed to this shift in the legal industry. Clients are increasingly looking for efficient and cost-effective solutions, and alternative legal service providers are filling that gap. And all that was a factor before the advent of ChatGPT or Goldman Sachs suggestion that AI could replace two-thirds of jobs in the United States and Europe with lawyers topping the list of "endangered species."[8]

----

7 Occupational Outlook Handbook, Bureau of Labor Statistics, U.S. Department of Labor, 15 Sept. 2021, https://www.bls.gov/ooh/legal/lawyers.htm#tab-6.

8 https://observer.com/2023/03/generative-a-i-may-replace-300-million-jobs-goldman-sachs-study/

As small firms struggle to compete, large firms continue to buy out smaller practices and merge into regional mega-firms. These firms are able to leverage their size and resources to invest in technology, take advantage of economies of scale, and earn greater name recognition and brand awareness. These firms are able to compete in ways that smaller practices simply cannot, making it increasingly difficult for solo practitioners and small firms to stay afloat.

As a final blow, the legal industry is facing new challenges in the form of changing regulations. Amendments to Rule 5.4 of the American Bar Association's Model Rules of Professional Conduct now make it possible for non-lawyers to share fees, which means that financial, tech, and marketing professionals are entering the competition as well.

This evolution means that not only are lawyers competing with other lawyers but they must also compete with the investment and influence of these other professionals who can bring additional expertise and resources to the table.

Facing the Realities

Are these realities harsh? Indeed. But, you **can** compete with these firms IF you take steps to remain competitive.

The Law Firm Growth Machine enables you to do just that.

Closing Arguments

- **Harsh Reality #1:** You aren't keeping up - Technology has become an integral part of the legal industry, and firms that have not embraced it are struggling to keep up with the demands of clients and competitors. Many firms have failed to adopt the right technology solutions, but it's not too late to change. With the help of technology, AI, and data-driven systems like The Law Firm Growth Machine, firms can save time and energy, empower their teams, and provide better service to their clients.

- **Harsh Reality #2**: You can't do this alone - Growth in a law firm requires collaboration across all teams. Operating in silos can create a false sense of achievement for each team, but it doesn't result in sustainable growth. The critical growth systems in your firm are Marketing, Intake, and Service, and it is important that each individual or team work beyond their respective roles. By investing in the right partners, facilitating communication between teams, and overseeing successful execution as the CEO, you can achieve growth.

- **Harsh Reality #3**: You don't know your numbers - Successfully facing challenges in the current environment requires data-driven decision-making, so you must know your numbers. Knowing the average value of a case, campaign conversion rate, and average acquisition cost are just a few examples of metrics that need to be tracked. The Law Firm Growth Machine has basic reporting and Key Performance Indicators (KPIs) built-in to empower teams, improve decision-making, and drive growth.

- **Harsh Reality #4**: It's Google's world. We're just living in it. - The power of Google in the digital world is immense and cannot be ignored. Google controls "near me" searches, maps, and customer reviews. To compete, businesses must appease the Google gods by soliciting feedback, responding to consumer requests, and feeding the algorithm.

- **Harsh Reality #5**: Your competition is increasing - The legal industry has been growing exponentially for decades, however, demand for traditional legal services has declined. Large law firms are buying out smaller practices, making it harder for solo practitioners and small firms to compete, while alternative service providers have taken a share of the traditional legal services market. Changes in regulation and technology are also impacting the industry further increasing competition for legal clients.

"

Success is neither magical nor mysterious. Success is the natural consequence of consistently applying basic fundamentals.

JIM ROHN

CHAPTER 4

THE KEY TO CONSISTENT GROWTH

If you haven't read James Clear's *Atomic Habits*, I recommend you add it to your list immediately.

It was one of the most impactful books of my career and one that I think of often when it comes to consulting attorneys on the small, consistent actions that compound over time and build a profitable and satisfying practice.

In his book, Clear writes about the underperforming British Cycling team. A century of mediocrity would end under new leadership focused on seeking every minute opportunity for improvement. From seat adjustments to replacing pillows, dialing in nutrition to optimizing racing suits, small changes added up to dramatic wins for the once-struggling team.

But, let's face it, that kind of consistent commitment to the most minuscule of details is hard to maintain when you aren't dealing with intense, competitive athletes (let alone while juggling needy clients and complex legal work).

That's exactly why building systems in your business is imperative to attaining your goals, and growth is no exception.

Your growth machine will be a powerful system built to ensure that micro-moments add up to a whole lot of momentum in your practice and make your firm unstoppable.

The Success is in the System

In *The E-Myth Revisited*, Michael Gerber noted, "Let the systems run the business. Let the people run the systems."

Given current conditions in the industry - intense competition, sky-rocketing prices, and shrinking margins - systemizing critical functions, including growth, has never been more important.

Why?

Because every signed case can have a dramatic impact on your bottom line and ultimately determine if you are in a position to grow.

I'm reminded of a conference I attended years ago. I was seated beside a commercial airline pilot, and we were talking about the importance of systems. He shared with me that if the airline industry was "merely" 99.99% effective in safely delivering their service promise, there would **still** be an astonishing four airline crashes every day.

Imagine!

Safely delivering passengers to their destination is quite literally a matter of life and death, so the airline industry has made an art of systemization and standardization. It's just that important.

If something is that important, it must be systemized. Full stop.

Not Just Any System... A Growth System!

Your law firm is likely staffed by highly capable and driven personnel, but our work is multi-faceted and our attention is often pulled from the task at hand. Any business that is consumer-driven and client-facing means that the day will be full of interruptions that distract us from our best intentions.

With that in mind, it is not only possible but extremely likely that you are **not** operating at 99.99% and crashing four metaphorical planes each day!

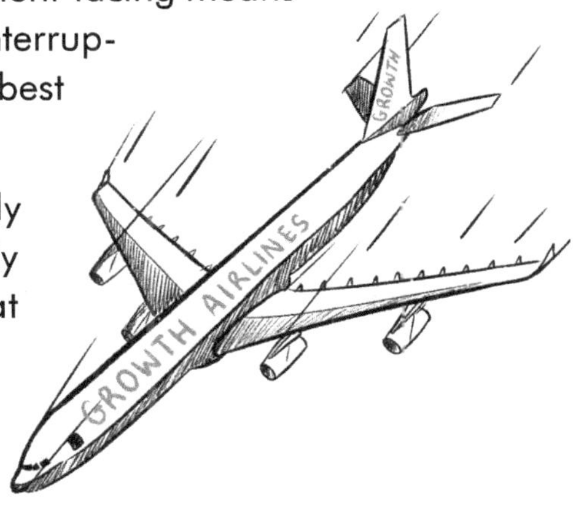

If you're going to be highly effective in growing your practice, you must implement a system to do so.

Chances are, you've considered growth to be a consequence of your other systems in your practice, from marketing to intake to case management or even good hiring. That's not entirely untrue as those systems are critical components of your growth system, but creating a system specifically for growth is as important as any of the other systems in your business.

A growth system, specifically, is a set of processes and procedures that are designed to increase the firm's revenue and/or expand its footprint. This includes a combination of marketing, intake, business development, and other elements that are used to attract new clients, maintain existing clients, and grow the firm's client base.

Like many of the other systems in your business, the growth system is a network of processes working together.

This is an important distinction, especially if you are operating a firm with a staff.

Let's consider the difference between a process and a system. A process is a series of steps taken to achieve a specific outcome. You may have a process for conducting an intake, for example. Regardless of who completes the intake, a series of tasks are completed in similar fashion every time.

A system, however, is defined as a network of processes working together. This is fundamental to understanding how your growth system should function.

Your growth system must centralize marketing, intake, service, and reputation - the systems that collectively drive the firm toward its growth objectives.

The growth system ensures (almost to airline standards, wink, wink!) effective execution of your growth strategy (which we will discuss in much greater detail in the next chapter) by providing structure and consistently performing processes designed to attain the growth objectives. In turn, your growth strategy guides the systems by providing a clear direction and purpose for their implementation.

Your law firm will benefit from implementing systems and probably already has. From hiring to case management, intake to file assignments, knowing the team assigned and the tactics they employ to run the system is empowering. Systems in your practice increase accuracy, accountability, and cost savings.

Similarly, a growth system will deliver countless benefits, none more so than operational efficiency as you and your team work together toward your growth objectives.

4 Benefits of an Effective Growth System

In service-based industries, growth comes from standing out personally with your clients, referral partners, and business network, and leveraging that reputation through your marketing efforts. To make time for that activity - especially if you are in a small or solo practice - you must increase efficiency in every way possible.

1. An effective growth system automates many of the repetitive and administrative tasks involved in managing a law firm's growth, such as lead capture, client acquisition, retention, and marketing efforts. This will free up employees' time and allow them to instead focus on more important tasks that machines cannot do, like cultivating meaningful relationships with clients and referral partners.

2. An effective growth system helps streamline the process of growing the law firm by providing a centralized location for all growth-related information and documentation, allowing employees to access and manage growth-related activities more efficiently. That collaboration is fundamental to driving growth.

3. An effective growth system generates performance data across the firm. When firms convert this data to intelligence, they are equipped to make better growth decisions that drive profits higher. Red flags are identified sooner. Growth opportunities become more apparent. You take growth to the next level.

4. Finally, an effective growth system increases efficiencies which should improve client satisfaction. And happy clients will enhance your reputation. While your reputation alone isn't exactly high-octane fuel for your growth machine, you can think of it as an essential additive that keeps your bearings lubricated and flywheel spinning.

Let me expand on that last point further:

A purpose-built growth system helps law firms improve their reputation by creating efficiencies that allow them the time to provide exceptional service, and exceptional service is an invitation for a stellar reputation. When happy clients share their experience with others, you improve your reach, enhance your reputation, and attract new business.

With every client interaction, there's an additional opportunity to build your brand, expand your reach, attract top talent, and ultimately, grow your practice - and growth is good.

A law firm that is growing and expanding is typically a more desirable place to work. Lawyers and other legal professionals are attracted to firms that are growing and offer opportunities for advancement, bringing with them a client base or personal following of their own which can lead to further growth.

A growing firm will also have the opportunity to specialize, inviting the opportunity to stand out in a particular competency, build a niche practice, or attract attention from a specific pool of prospects.

In short, a good reputation is paramount to growth.

The Consequences of Inadequate Systems

Without proper systems in place, your law firm risks negative consequences that can impact your team, reputation, revenue, and even your bar license and well-being. Inadequate systems can result in delays in completing tasks, overlooking crucial information, missing deadlines and court appearances, and losing out on opportunities that require a timely response.

As an attorney, failing to deliver can have severe consequences, including dismissal of a case or default judgment, legal malpractice lawsuits, and career-ending effects.

It's no wonder case management software became so essential to operating an effective practice!

Shouldn't your growth carry the same level of insurance?

In the current "buyers' economy," even failing to respond quickly to a *prospect* can lead to a poor reputation and a lack of referral business, ensuring your client acquisition costs will remain high.

In fact, costs in general are sure to increase without adequate systems.

Given the shrinking margins many attorneys are currently experiencing, controlling costs is exceptionally important to growing a practice. Failure to do so will directly inhibit growth, limiting the potential for new opportunities and the ability to compete with other firms.

A business that fails to grow will struggle to attract talent, invest in new technology that in time becomes standard technology, will struggle financially, and, ultimately, lose to the bigger players in the market with the purse to acquire and take on cases that can be expensive to litigate but lucrative to win.

Do you remember life before your Case Management Software?

Now, imagine that you could implement a system to drive growth and transform your business as profoundly as your CMS has transformed your case management!

Recall a period of time before Case Management Software was a practice standard.

Back then, lawyers managed their cases using manual processes such as paper files, calendars, and reminders. Dare I say, a few veteran attorneys had yellow sticky notes trimming the edge of an IBM.

Managing cases in this pre-CMS way often involved a significant amount of manual labor, such as copying and filing documents, scheduling appointments, and sending reminders. Case progress, deadlines, and client communication were all tracked manually, which could be both time-consuming and error-prone.

Confusion and inconsistencies were commonplace. Collaboration between lawyers and team members was often difficult as information had to be manually shared and passed along.

The result of all of this manual work was higher costs and decreased productivity, directly affecting the bottom line.

The case management system made your firm stronger. In fact, I bet you wish you had adopted a CMS even sooner, and I'll even double down that you'll feel no different once you implement a growth system. Just as the CMS brought strength and order to file management, a growth system will positively affect your practice in ways you'll only wish you had implemented sooner.

Overcoming Your System Blockers

I know many of you might be thinking that it's too costly, or too rigid, or your firm is too small, or any number of objections that prevent you from owning this challenge in this moment and building your growth system. But, you're a lawyer! And lawyers do hard things, beating the competition time and again as the studies have shown.

However, as so many of you undoubtedly love a good argument, let's tackle each of those concerns independently for a moment.

1. Systems are too expensive

Perhaps it stems from James' influence given his background in finance, but I've been beating the drum for years about *business investments* versus *business expenses* in law firms. In a book I wrote specifically on intake, I made the case that paying a certain premium for talent would prove a better investment than "saving" on a more affordable candidate.

If you pay up to hire someone who has better experience, professionalism, demeanor, and work ethic, do you think he or she will sign more clients and attract more business to your firm than someone who may require a lower wage but prove less effective at signing new cases, generating referral business, and being an ambassador for your firm?

If the difference between the high-dollar talent and the more affordable applicant equates to $15,000 annually, do you think the higher-caliber employee could make up for that difference in new cases?

Such assessments are necessary when it comes to driving growth for your business, and again, given the premium price of your services, a slight edge could actually make a huge dent in your goals.

Invest in your business!

Now, that said, you may be surprised to find that building a growth system utilizing the framework this book provides isn't actually a costly investment at all if you leverage technology. Hiring someone to work in-house and manually do all the work required to prioritize growth, however, certainly would be. While technology can bridge that gap, it's not lost on us that the technical expertise and time costs are hefty.

That's why we've taken a decade of experience with law practices and the lessons learned from high-dollar consulting engagements to give smaller firms the ability to plug into our system and, in as little as 30 days, generate the momentum that will sustain and grow a practice.

2. Systems are for large firms only

Wrong! Systems are especially important in small law firms that want to compete with larger firms, and, again, growth is no exception.

Let's revisit Scott whose story we shared in Chapter 1. Scott is now actively competing with well-established firms in a very large market. Why? Because he has a system in place, ensuring that he can capture, convert, and leverage his existing business to generate more business, investing wisely in growth.

Small law firms have limited resources, including time and staff, just as Scott did initially. Here's what a growth system was able to accomplish for him:

- Streamline processes and make the most of his resources, enabling him to work more efficiently and effectively.
- Scale up operations and take on more clients. He was able to effectively hire and train staff to work within his system.
- Provide a consistent level of service to clients, which was critical in building his reputation and attracting new business.

- Identify his best lead sources and control costs to maximize profitability, enabling him to compete with larger firms.

Not yet convinced?

I'll share with you the argument that prevented me from taking the time and energy necessary to implement robust systems into my business operations sooner:

3. Systems are too rigid

James Clear, again, won me over on this argument. Creativity and systems can work together, and it is not necessarily true that some people are "too creative" to use systems. In fact, implementing systems can enhance creativity and innovation in a law firm.

We have to again acknowledge the time-savings that systems offer. If we enable technology to handle much of the tedious work that stifles creativity, we free our mental space to take on more interesting and profitable work. I prefer to focus on the work that machines can't do - like relationship building and client care - that differentiate the practice (and the attorney) from others. Systems can help to provide a clear focus and direction for a law firm, which can free up creative energy to be directed toward solving specific problems or developing new ideas.

With the ability for systems to generate data outputs, exploring new ideas can become a meaningful endeavor in the practice. Systems can provide a framework for experimentation and testing, which can lead to innovation and creativity that can be evaluated as potential solutions for existing challenges or growth avenues. Further, systems can facilitate collaboration among team members, which can also lead to greater creativity.

Given the benefits and risks of failing to systemize something as fundamental to the health of your practice as growth, it's time to ask yourself:

Why don't you have a growth system?

Closing Arguments

- You need a growth system. Systems are imperative for any critical functions in a practice, and for attorneys seeking to grow, a growth system must be employed. A growth system is a network of processes and procedures designed to increase a firm's revenue and expand its footprint.

- An effective growth system increases efficiency, accuracy, accountability, and cost savings. It automates repetitive tasks and streamlines processes to enable teams to invest their time in high-value work. A purpose-built system also improves client satisfaction and reputation, which will attract new business and top talent.

- Good systems result in better service, more satisfied clients, and an improved reputation. Data outputs from systems inform decision-making that can improve revenue.

- Failing to implement a growth system is more costly than building one. Without systems in place for critical functions like growth, law firms will struggle to manage their workload and workflow. This can lead to legal malpractice and a poor reputation, resulting in a lack of referral business and high client acquisition costs. Without systems, it will be difficult to provide exceptional service, retain clients, and attract new ones.

- Implementing a growth system is as important as a case management system, and failure to do so will hinder the growth of the firm and make it difficult to compete in the current market.

- Small law firms must employ systems in order to compete with larger firms.

- Implementing systems will help to enhance creativity and innovation in a law firm. Systems provide structure and a framework for creativity to flourish by saving time and allowing individuals to focus on more interesting and profitable work.

"

A fool with a tool is still a fool.

GRADY BOOCH

CHAPTER 5

THE CATCH

Throughout your time as an attorney, you have likely implemented systems to solve problems, and, after the last chapter, you are thoroughly convinced that, indeed, you need a growth system.

But, there's a fundamental problem with how most law firms approach systems which makes implementing a growth system particularly challenging.

Most firms think a "system" is simply a matter of purchasing a plethora of software tools specific to each department or individual and letting them get on with it only to be disappointed by the results.

Those aren't systems. Those are tools. A system must capture a strategy and make it more efficient to execute that strategy.

Without a well-defined strategy that every team member understands and is bought into, your system will fail.

A system without a strategy is like a vision without a plan... It's a dream!

Defining A Growth Strategy

Some growth strategies are familiar to you and are particularly effective as they generate momentum for the business.

Take Walmart and Amazon for example.

Walmart's business strategy is focused on providing low prices to customers through cost leadership and operational efficiency, leveraging economies of scale, purchasing power, and operational efficiency to offer lower prices than competitors.

Amazon's business strategy is centered on providing an exceptionally wide selection of products, fast delivery, and excellent customer service by investing in logistics, delivery infrastructure, and e-commerce capabilities.

Both companies are known for their efforts to meet consumer demands for value and accessibility and also have been making efforts to reduce their environmental impact.

Conversely, some brands seek not to enjoy mass popularity through value but, rather, to attract fewer clients with much higher-end products.

Under Armour's business strategy is focused on providing high-performance athletic gear and apparel for athletes.

The company seeks to differentiate itself from competitors by offering innovative and high-quality products that are designed to improve athletic performance.

They achieve this by investing in research and development to create new and advanced materials and technologies, such as moisture-wicking fabrics, and by collaborating with elite athletes to design and test products.

The company then focuses on building its brand image and creating strong relationships with athletes and sports teams to increase brand awareness and customer loyalty without having to compete on price. Customers, drawn to the brands favored by elite athletes, eagerly pay up.

You may even note that some companies, Rolex for example, drive their growth by focusing on exclusivity, even to the point of generating years-long wait lists to acquire their product!

Supreme, a streetwear brand known for its limited edition releases of clothing and accessories, releases a new collection each week with a limited number of items in each release. The limited release creates a sense of scarcity and exclusivity around the brand and has helped to build a cult-like following.

In all of these examples, the actions of the business not only affect growth directly but they ultimately fuel further growth.

The "Must Employ" Law Firm Strategy

As an attorney, there are several business strategies that you can employ to propel growth for your practice. The best strategy for your firm will depend on your practice area, skills, team, mission, vision, and objectives. Your strategy must take into consideration the resources (human, financial, and practical) available to execute it, and the challenges you face in your market.

But there is one strategy that is plainly required of any client-serviced-based business that, ignored, will at best fail to generate new business from existing business and at worst will sabotage all other efforts to grow the business.

A reputation-enhancing strategy based on relationship-building

Building strong relationships with clients and referral partners is crucial for professional service providers. This can be achieved by providing excellent customer service, being responsive to client needs, going above and beyond to meet their expectations, and delivering results. Relationship-building also extends beyond clients to the community at large, cultivating a good reputation and association locally. Investing in these relationships can be both a direct line to growth (referrals) as well as a slow-burner (reputation-enhancing).

The strategy is profoundly simple but can distinguish your firm from your competitors. Create raving fans of your clients who then become advocates for your firm. Advocates will drive new business to your practice in the form of leads that you convert to clients, winning the opportunity to satisfy with your service again!

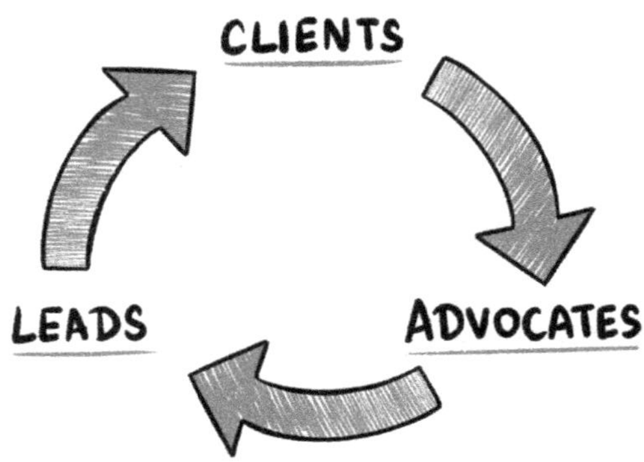

But here's the catch. Who has time for this?

Given the countless demands on individuals and teams, investing in relationships can feel like an implausibility. But there is a solution that is necessary for firms looking to remain competitive in this market. We absolutely must achieve operational efficiencies by leaning on technology.

The Law Firm Growth Machine is teeming with time-saving features, but where you reinvest that time is what will compel growth. And that is investing in your relationships.

The cornerstone of sound relationships is trust. And establishing trust with prospects and clients requires three elements at a minimum:

- **Rapport**
- **Responsiveness**
- **Results**

Here's how the Law Firm Growth Machine supports your efforts to build good relationships that will result in the flywheel effect:

1. Rapport building takes time. By eliminating manual tasks as much as possible, intake professionals are better able to spend time listening to and connecting with prospects.

2. Responsiveness is consistently ranked among consumers' greatest frustrations with law firms. Leveraging automation informs prospects that we are aware of their inquiry and will reach out to them as soon as we are able. That single message alone is often enough to halt an online prospect's search for an attorney.

3. Trust requires that you deliver on your promise. Your clients expect you to achieve the best outcome and by showcasing your success by means of online reviews and client testimonials, you are able to offer prospects reassurance that their problems can be solved by working with you.

By implementing a system that improves efficiency on tasks that don't require human interaction, you are able to reinvest that time where it matters and that is in relationship building, the primary function of human interaction.

Law firms pay handsomely to generate leads for their practice. These leads must be more than transactional or you will forever find yourself on the relentless treadmill of paying up for leads only to have to do it again and again and again.

But if each lead becomes an advocate for your firm, that investment in a single lead can net results that pay for years to come.

Look, there are an abundance of law firms in countless corners of this country from coast to coast. You are likely practicing in one of them. To differentiate yourself as a practice you must do several things:

1. You need to streamline in every way possible to make time to do the real business of serving clients.

2. You need to consider good service a minimum standard and differentiate yourself in the client experience.

3. You need to create raving fans who want to help you as much as you've helped them.

Now here's the beauty of building a relationship instead of merely serving a client. A relationship by nature results in a mutual benefit to those in said relationship.

When you provide the level of service, care, and results that I know you can given the operational efficiencies of your growth system, your clients will feel compelled to repay you with their endorsement, their glowing review, and their referrals. A true relationship is one in which each party benefits, which makes asking for reviews and referrals effortless. Your clients will enhance your reputation when they feel you have helped them.

Reputation Matters

Your reputation is, and always has been, invaluable. Syrian-born writer, Publilius Syrus, believed to have lived in the 1st century, knew even then that it was "more valuable than money." Twenty centuries later, this holds true. Your reputation enters every room before you and remains long after you exit. And as Warren Buffett noted, it can take decades to build and a few poor moments to destroy. In the age of the internet, and particularly in the consumer-driven, share-everything, viral world we live in, this has never been truer.

The internet has dramatically changed the way that people manage and grow their reputation, and for service providers, this means having to actively work to control the narrative. Firms that recognize the value of reputation stand to benefit over those that ignore this aspect of their practice and the impact it can have on business development efforts.

While the idea that the customer is always right has been around since the birth of the department store, this has particular implications in the modern era where consumers aren't only being told the finely cultivated marketing message and a few hand-selected testimonials, but speaking directly to previous clients about their experience in open forums like social media.

Research has shown that negative emotions can be felt more strongly than positive emotions. Studies have found that people tend to remember negative events more vividly and for a longer period of time than positive events. This 'negativity bias' suggests that negative experiences may leave a stronger emotional imprint and cause individuals to take action, like leaving a scathing review, as a result.

That said, it's imperative that you not leave acquiring positive reviews to chance. Doing so is an invitation for negative feedback completely unbalanced by the positive commentary of satisfied clients and raving advocates.

And prospective clients want this "social proof" about your services from their peers.

The Era of Social Proof

Social proof is a psychological phenomenon in which people look to the actions and opinions of others to determine their own behavior. It refers to the idea that people are more likely to conform to the actions of a group or to follow the opinions of relative peers, especially when they are uncertain about the correct course of action, like which attorney to hire.

By highlighting the popularity of an attorney, for example, by showcasing positive reviews or testimonials, trust in the individual and perceived value is increased.

When you demonstrate that others have had positive experiences with your firm, you can increase the likelihood that potential clients will choose their offerings over those of their competitors.

And before we dive into how you generate this social proof, even if you have an incredibly busy practice or lack the staff to deal with these ancillary tasks, I want to point out a few realities every attorney must consider when it comes to both safeguarding and augmenting your reputation.

Reach: The Ripple Effect of Online Reputation

First is reach. Whereas the griping letter of an unhappy client may have once found its way to your mailbox decades ago, it is unlikely that same letter ended up in the newspaper and got plastered up and down Main Street.

That's not the case anymore.

Negative reviews can reach far and wide from your local community, to your referral network, your peer community (that is often rating each other in other reputation-enhancing efforts such as SuperLawyers or Legal Elite), to your alumni network.

Impact: The Unforgiven Consequences

Secondly, these reviews travel quickly and can be part of the "permanent record" prospects will find online. Whereas time may have once healed a multitude of reputational sins, if the matter finds life online, it can live forever.

This is all part of what prospective clients will find when they search your name or firm online, so controlling the narrative around your reputation is an important part of what search results will unveil.

Remember, it's Google's world; we're just living in it.

The bottom line here is this: You must actively work to maintain a positive online reputation.

Do not leave this to chance.

A good reputation resulting from authentic relationships proudly amplified, will help grow your business, drive down acquisition costs, and attract new clients.

We're going to show you how to systemize this strategy so that you can reinvest your time where it matters most and achieve the Holy Grail of law firm growth... The Flywheel Effect.

Closing Arguments

- A system without a strategy is doomed to fail. Any service-based business requires an investment in relationships to generate business and enhance one's reputation.
- A successful growth system must capture the strategy, centralize key elements affecting growth, and break down silos between teams.
- Building strong relationships with clients and referral partners is crucial for professional service providers. Therefore, relationship-building must be a core component of the strategy for all law firms.
- Building trust with prospects and clients through rapport, responsiveness, and results is necessary for creating a mutually beneficial relationship. By streamlining tasks and reinvesting time in building relationships, law firms can differentiate themselves, provide excellent service, and create raving fans who will endorse, give glowing reviews, and refer them to others.
- While a good reputation has always been important, the internet has changed the reach and impact of reputation and the way people manage and amplify theirs.

- Negative emotions are felt more strongly than positive emotions and negative experiences can leave a stronger emotional imprint, leading to negative reviews which can spread quickly and become part of the permanent online record. To counteract this, firms must actively work to generate positive reviews, which can provide social proof and increase trust in the business.

- Social proof is a powerful psychological phenomenon that can be leveraged in growing your firm. By demonstrating that others have had positive experiences, potential clients are more likely to choose their offerings over competitors.

PART TWO

What You Need to Get Started

A WORD FROM JAMES

In Part 1, Kerri helped you conceptualize The Law Firm Growth Machine and provided context for building a growth machine of your own. She expertly made the case for why having the right systems in place is a cornerstone of sustainable growth for your law firm. She explained why systems are so important and why failing to systemize will lead to problems further down the line. However, she warned in Chapter 5 not to build systems without a solid strategy. Without a clear plan in place, she cautioned, even the best systems will fail.

Now, In Part 2, we strategize so we can later systemize.

In this section, Kerri explains the concept of the flywheel and why achieving the flywheel effect is so important for delivering consistent growth for law firms. The flywheel effect is a self-reinforcing loop that generates momentum and growth over time. By creating a flywheel effect in your law firm, you can build a business that continues to grow and thrive, even as you scale.

Next, Kerri revists the relationship-building strategy introduced in Chapter 5. In the legal industry, relationships are important. A law firm's success often depends on one's ability to build and maintain strong relationships with clients, referral sources, and even competitors. A solid reputation is paramount to building these relationships, which is why The Law Firm Growth Flywheel kicks off by generating reputation-enhancing reviews.

The combination of relationships and reputation is leveraged to generate attention for the firm. Attention helps generate leads that are captured and retained as clients. Investing in the client experience then further enhances one's reputation and garners more 5-star reviews. And so, the flywheel spins.

While this process is simple, Kerri has often found that firms struggle to implement it, largely due to the lack of a plan that unites all departments and their efforts, which is required to consistently manage these growth-related tasks. To help law firms overcome this challenge and seamlessly achieve the flywheel effect, Kerri introduces the Flywheel 5T (F5T) framework.

The framework is designed to align your teams and implement your growth strategy effectively. Kerri breaks down each of these five Ts and provides practical guidance on how to use them to achieve your growth goals.

Finally, Kerri emphasizes the importance of a strong brand, the right people, investing in marketing, and adopting a CEO mindset. These fundamental elements are all essential for ambitious firms seeking to build a growth machine that can take the firm to the next level.

In summary, Part 2 of The Law Firm Growth Machine is all about implementing a growth strategy for law firms. Kerri covers the importance of a relationship-driven strategy, the flywheel effect, and the F5T framework your firm can use today.

"

Momentum is a leader's best friend.

JOHN C. MAXWELL

CHAPTER 6

GENERATING THE FLYWHEEL EFFECT

In his iconic book, *Good to Great*, Jim Collins draws a parallel between a mechanical flywheel and the growth of a business. Both require a tremendous amount of effort to set in motion initially, but those efforts, delivered consistently, compound over time and create near unstoppable momentum.

If you've been running your practice for some time, you can likely recall the tremendous hustle of those early days, or if you are fairly new to practice you may be wondering if your efforts will ever pay off.

They can.

You just need to create the flywheel effect in your practice, an effect so powerful and yet so simple that it has been adopted by some of the world's most influential and successful companies.

Collins explains that the flywheel effect is a system "relentlessly pushing a giant, heavy flywheel turn upon turn, building momentum until a point of breakthrough and beyond.... Once that breakthrough occurs, the momentum of the stored energy propels the mechanism forward with a minimal amount of effort. Now, you no longer have to work so hard because the dynamic momentum takes over and makes the work easier."

Flywheels in Motion

Jeff Bezos recognized the power of the flywheel early on when building his Amazon enterprise—and hired Jim Collins to help Amazon identify its own flywheel. For Amazon, it was focusing on economies of scale. The company was generating interest by offering low prices, so they doubled down on that. They didn't try to go back and change everything.

Amazon's flywheel looked like this:

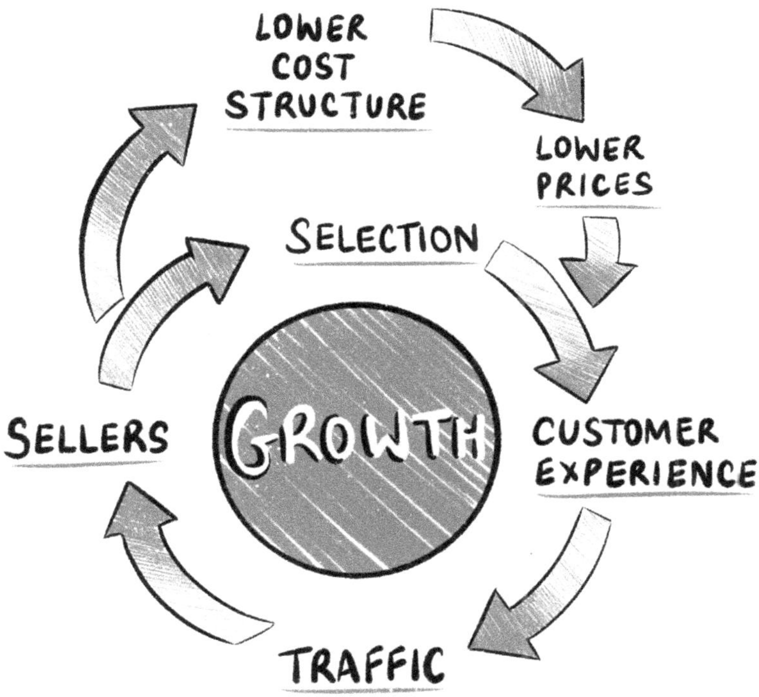

- Lower prices led to more customer visits.
- More customer visits led to an increase in sales.
- An increase in sales led to an ability to attract third-party sellers to the site.
- Attracting third-party sellers to the site enabled Amazon to obtain better pricing on fulfillment.
- Obtaining better pricing on fulfillment drove down prices.
- Lower costs attracted more customers to the site.

As a result, Amazon was able to create better service by growing bigger.

Vanguard is another company that successfully set its flywheel in motion and benefited from the economies of scale (offering lower-cost mutual funds). Vanguard's flywheel is:

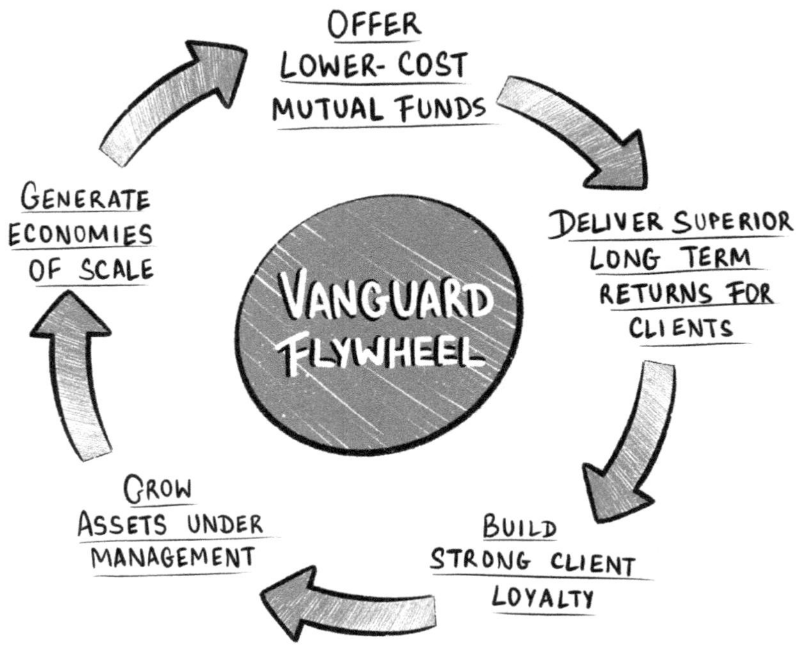

- Offering lower-cost mutual funds for investors led to better long-term returns.
- Delivering better long-term returns led to investor loyalty.

- Investor loyalty increased assets under Vanguard's management.
- Increased assets enabled Vanguard to drive down mutual funds prices.

In the early 1990s, Littler Mendelson, a California-based labor and employment law firm, was dealing with competitors undercutting the market. The firm needed a new strategy in order to compete and expand beyond their local area, so it looked at Jim Collins' flywheel to see how it might apply to them.

With the flywheel in mind, the firm developed a strategy and built a knowledge management library and internal webpage that its lawyers could access for updated answers to recurring problems in employment and labor law issues.

Littler Mendelson believed that, by developing a subspeciality and reinvesting in that subspeciality, the firm could become a resource for other attorneys who needed that support. It also would expand Littler Mendelson's network and grow its reputation as experts in the field of employment and labor law.

And it worked.

Littler Mendelson attracts people who are "thrilled about serving clients, which compounds their growth." In addition, "The compensation system uniquely rewards the sharing of business and servicing of clients. And that's the fundamental glue for bonding people together."

As you can see, the magic of the flywheel is in its simplicity.

We've created The Law Firm Growth Machine to help attorneys generate the flywheel effect. It systemizes a proven strategy to ensure consistency that will enable your efforts to compound over time.

The Law Firm Growth Flywheel

Our flywheel concept represents a self-sustaining and reinforcing loop of growth whereby a growth system creates efficiencies that enables firms to invest more time into serving clients. Increased client satisfaction enhances the firm's reputation, which, in turn, generates more opportunities.

Here's what the Law Firm Growth Flywheel looks like:

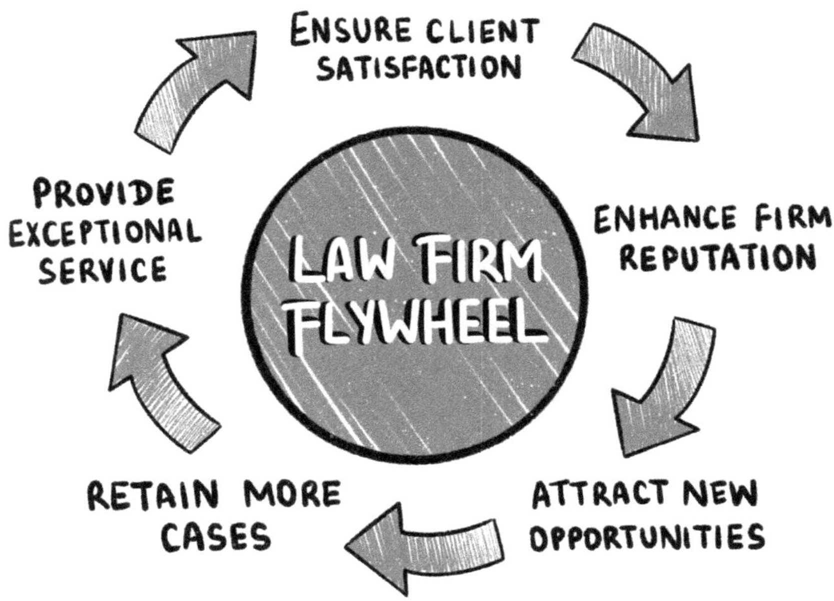

- An exceptional client experience leads to an enhanced firm reputation.
- An enhanced reputation attracts new opportunities.
- New opportunities leads to more signed cases.
- Increased revenue allows for investment in the client experience to ensure both client satisfaction and continued momentum of your flywheel.

In short, leads become clients. Great service improves satisfaction so that clients become advocates. Amplifying the firm's reputation increases opportunities ensuring that strangers become leads.

Note here that there must be an investment - even if that investment is only of time - in the client experience to overcome what we previously identified as a common growth challenge - that as client volume increases, the client experience declines. Overcoming this challenge requires investment and the effective use of technology. It's important to highlight that this is indeed an investment - not an expense. An exceptional client experience will generate additional attention and drive referral business.

James and I have studied the traditional marketing funnel in struggling firms and have recognized a fundamental flaw: the money invested in acquiring clients is purely transactional. New business does not lead to additional business. The only way new business can be generated is to spend more. Spending more doesn't *necessarily* result in more cases - but it does result in more work that could overwhelm the team and further impede acquisition.

When you shift to a strategy in which your business fuels business, you effectively get off the treadmill of feeding the machine at the top of a funnel to spit out business at the other end only to have to feed the funnel again.

A flywheel model shifts movement so that each interaction fuels growth and presents an opportunity to build your reputation and attract new business, effectively driving down costs as you do.

Generating the flywheel effect in your business requires that you identify and invest in ways that amplify your strengths.

But remember, the magic of the flywheel is in the irony of "momentum." What the flywheel lacks in that BIG moment it makes up for in the compounding effect of all those micro-moments. Recall the British cycling team that James Clear describes in *Atomic Habits*. You must build systems to execute your strategy with that same elite, athlete-level of commitment.

That's what The Law Firm Growth Machine is - it's a system wrapped around your strategy to ensure those micro-moments add up to a whole lot of momentum in your practice.

5 Steps To Setting Your Flywheel in Motion

If you are ready to push the flywheel you'll need to start with this simple, 5-step approach to generate momentum in your practice.

1. Solcit Feedback

Start by reaching out to past/existing clients, referral partners, and others familiar with your quality of work to generate reviews, and ensure seeking reviews are a routine part of your practice.

Online reviews can have an immediate, positive impact on your business by increasing its visibility and reach immediately, attracting new customers and building trust through improved credibility.

Reviews can also help with search engine optimization as search engines use them as a ranking factor. Remember, it's Google's world, and Google puts a high premium on consumer satisfaction.

Positive online reviews can also influence purchasing decisions, resulting in increased conversions and clients for the practice in the era of social proof and transparency.

2. Amplify Advocates

Next, leverage these reviews to generate more attention for your firm, from consumers as well as referral partners, by replying and posting on social media, Google Business Profiles, your blog, and more.

All marketing efforts begin with awareness of your business. This can be a time-consuming endeavor though and is one that often gets overlooked when business grows hectic.

Building a sustainable business means committing to the long curve of "awareness," not just the short-term successes of "activation" (think PPC, LSA, "call now" style) campaigns.

This is why employing technology and automation to make effortless work of such tasks is imperative in ensuring the consistency that really transforms your business and results in the flywheel effect.

Encouraging clients to leave reviews and responding to both positive and negative reviews highlights your firm's engagement and helps prospects understand your client experience. This can improve your firm's service delivery and help create a dialogue with the community that increases awareness of your firm and generates leads.

3. Systemize Intake

Capture and convert more of these leads on platforms such as the website, and ensure all communication with the brand is centralized so that nothing slips through the cracks.

Building awareness of your firm through reviews will help drive visitors to your site, and you want to ensure that every opportunity to build a relationship with a prospect is provided.

Conversion tools on your website and social media can dramatically increase your opportunities and build authority and trust with your community.

Centralizing all lead activity in a single platform ensures no lead is left behind.

Engage leads immediately, and follow up regularly until that prospect is booked for a consultation or engaged on a call.

Engaging and following up with leads can be time-consuming, but it can have a significant effect on your firm's success.

Employing a system that supports your conversion efforts, investing in training your intake team, and providing prospects with every opportunity to partake of your services could dramatically transform your growth trajectory.

4. Invest in Client Service

Build a relationship with existing clients so they have a good experience with your firm from the moment they become a client to the time their case is settled, which, in turn, should ensure more positive reviews, more firm ambassadors, and an enhanced reputation for the firm.

As legal services become more commoditized, it becomes more difficult to differentiate yourself and compel prospects to choose your firm to solve their legal challenges. It is challenging to stand out and attract clients and to convince them to pay a premium for your services, but we have to try!

Providing exceptional service can help to build strong relationships with clients, establish a positive reputation, and differentiate your firm from competitors, all of which will help drive down the cost of acquisition.

Effective use of technology is a critical element in shifting where attorneys spend their time. Clients expect prompt and effective communication, clear and concise advice, and an attorney with a deep understanding of their needs and goals, and they are very vocal when they don't get it!

The right tools to communicate with clients, save time, and support your firm's efforts to provide exceptional service can demonstrate your firm's commitment to client satisfaction. This can lead to long-term relationships and increased referrals as well as more of those all-important, five-star reviews that enhance the firm's reputation and make it more attractive to potential clients and top talent.

5. Monitor Client Satisfaction

It is important to monitor client satisfaction throughout the engagement as a key step in setting your law firm's flywheel in motion.

By tracking client satisfaction throughout a client's engagement, you can gain valuable insights into what is working well and what areas may need improvement.

Regularly soliciting feedback allows the firm to address any concerns or issues as they arise, ensuring satisfaction and increasing the likelihood of positive reviews and referrals.

Continuously improving the client experience can result in a self-sustaining flywheel effect, where positive client experiences lead to more positive reviews, referrals, and business growth.

Advocates generate attention for the firm. Attention generates opportunities. Opportunities result in leads. Leads convert to clients. Happy clients become advocates.

And so, the flywheel spins!

Closing arguments

- The flywheel effect is a self-sustaining and reinforcing loop of growth that accelerates over time. To create the flywheel effect in a business, the focus should be on leveraging the strengths of the business to build momentum rather than fixing weaknesses.

- The Law Firm Growth Strategy can be quickly implemented and generates momentum at no cost. By committing to the details and building a system around the strategy, attorneys can ensure that small improvements add up to significant momentum in the practice.

- The 5 Steps of to set your flywheel in motion are:

  - **Solicit feedback.** Generate reviews beginning with your existing client base, and ensure generating reviews are a routine part of your practice.

  - **Amplify advocates.** Leverage these reviews to generate more attention for your firm by replying and posting on social media, Google Business Profiles, your blog, and more.

  - **Systemize your intake.** Capture and convert more of these leads on platforms such as the website, and ensure all communication with the brand is centralized so nothing slips through the cracks.

  - **Invest in client service.** Build relationships with clients so they have a good experience with your firm from the moment they become a client to the time their case is settled, which, in turn, should ensure more positive reviews and an enhanced reputation for the firm.

- **Monitor client satisfaction.** Gain valuable insights, address concerns, ensure satisfaction, and increase the likelihood of positive reviews and referrals.

✲ Attention from advocates generates opportunities. Opportunities result in leads. Leads convert to clients. Happy clients become advocates. Advocates generate attention for the firm, keeping the flywheel spinning.

"

Strategy is not the consequence of planning, but the opposite: its starting point.

HENRY MINTZBERG

CHAPTER 7

THE FLYWHEEL 5T FRAMEWORK

As CEO of your law firm, driving your growth strategy while also driving case strategies, referral relationships, professional networks, employee engagement, etc.... well, you can see how easily the details can slip.

That's why outlining the process and systemizing the strategy is so important.

Let's revisit the strategy that will generate the flywheel effect:

If you can successfully manage that, you can generate new leads that will push the flywheel and build momentum for your practice with each turn.

In our consulting engagements, James and I would ask ourselves the following questions as we sought to create the flywheel effect for our consulting clients:

- What were we trying to achieve?
- Who would be responsible for overseeing each aspect of the process?
- Who would be responsible for executing?
- What tools would those individuals need to perform to the highest standard?
- How would we hold people accountable?
- How would we measure performance?
- How would we communicate among those tasked with implementing the strategy?

We found that these tasks come down to three departments: Marketing, Intake, and Client Service, and while each team had unique goals, requirements, and approaches, we still needed a common language to collaborate across these departments.

What James and I created is a framework you can use to plan and execute your growth strategy and generate the flywheel effect. We call it the Flywheel 5T, or F5T for short. This framework will help you identify the elements that will set your flywheel in motion.

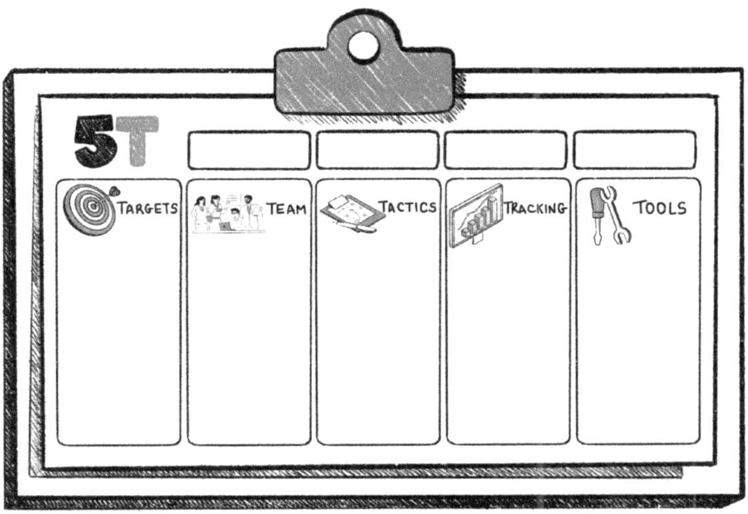

The 5Ts are as follows:

- **Targets**: What is the goal that we are reaching toward?
- **Team**: Who will execute, oversee, and ultimately be held accountable for attaining the goal?
- **Tactics**: What tactics will the team employ to achieve the goals?
- **Tracking**: How will we measure progress toward these goals?
- **Tools**: What tools will be required to reach these goals?

To set the flywheel in motion, leadership must identify all 5Ts as they relate to marketing, intake, and client service.

Let's take a closer look at each.

Targets: Setting the Standards for Growth

Targets are critical for each area of the business as they serve as a clear and concise definition of what the team is striving to achieve. Without well-defined targets, it is difficult to understand their objectives and work towards a common goal.

Targets are as important for busy practices who may just come in and grind aimlessly as they are for smaller practices who need to strive toward that mark. Having clear targets enables the individuals and teams to prioritize and allocate resources effectively.

Finding ways to bring a team together toward that common goal is an added benefit, so be sure to not only set targets for individuals but shared targets for teams. Aligning their efforts increases the chances of success and reduces the risk of wasting time and resources on irrelevant activities (not to mention building a culture of teamwork).

Your targets serve as a motivator for the team, giving them a sense of purpose and encouraging them to work harder to achieve the defined goals. When targets are met, the team is able to see the tangible results of their efforts and feel a sense of accomplishment. This, in turn, boosts morale and fosters a culture of continuous improvement.

By setting achievable targets, your departments can work towards creating a culture of excellence and continuous improvement.

Team: Defining Roles & Responsibilities

Defining roles and assembling a strong team are critical components in executing your strategy and meeting firm objectives. A clear understanding of who will be responsible for different tasks ensures that everyone is working towards those common goals and targets, reducing the risk of missed tasks, duplicated effort, or confusion.

This can be especially challenging in smaller firms where you may not be able to specialize roles and tasks as you like. Even so, defining what hat (or hats) will be worn by whom is an investment in long-term success.

Never assume who will assume a task!

It reminds me of a little poem of warning I recited for my children when they passed the buck as little ones:

> *This is a little story about four people named Everybody, Somebody, Anybody, and Nobody.*
>
> *There was an important job to be done, and Everybody was sure that Somebody would do it.*
>
> *Anybody could have done it, but Nobody did it.*
>
> *Somebody got angry about that because it was Everybody's job.*
>
> *Everybody thought that Anybody could do it, but Nobody realized that Everybody wouldn't do it.*
>
> *It ended up that Everybody blamed Somebody when Nobody did what Anybody could have done.*

Having a well-defined team helps to ensure accountability. Each team member knows what they are responsible for and can be held accountable for their actions, and people need responsibility, a sense of empowerment, and purpose! All of these increase motivation and a sense of accomplishment when they hit the mark. You're the CEO of your firm, and driving your team, building cohesion, is an important factor in your firm's pursuit of success.

When individuals know what is expected of them, you'll have a better work environment, sparing employees the blame game of who should have done what nobody owned.

Don't underestimate the power of the people in your organization. It's something we'll discuss again in Chapter 8, but this is a good time to remind attorneys that your firm is as strong as the people you employ.

As James taught me early on in building our business: Hire slow. Fire fast.

If you want a professional practice, employ professional people, and compensate them accordingly. Like marketing, this will not be an expense but an investment.

I'll also add something my father repeated frequently in his professional role: if your organization depends on any one person, fire that person immediately. Turns out, it was Henry Ford of assembly line manufacturing magic who is responsible for the quote, but a legend all the same in this author's eyes.

Defining roles, and having others know what those around them do, is an exercise in risk mitigation. Remember again the advice of Michael Gerber:

> **"Let the systems run the business. Let the people run the systems."**

Don't forget the importance of communication among teams in executing your strategy. Regular check-ins and updates help to keep everyone on track and aware of progress and can also help to identify and address potential roadblocks before they become major obstacles. Teams that communicate well are also more likely to foster a positive work environment, which can improve morale and increase motivation, helping teams build bonds that make them more inclined to support each other's efforts, all to the benefit of the bottom line and long-term success.

Tactics: Identifying the Best Route to Growth

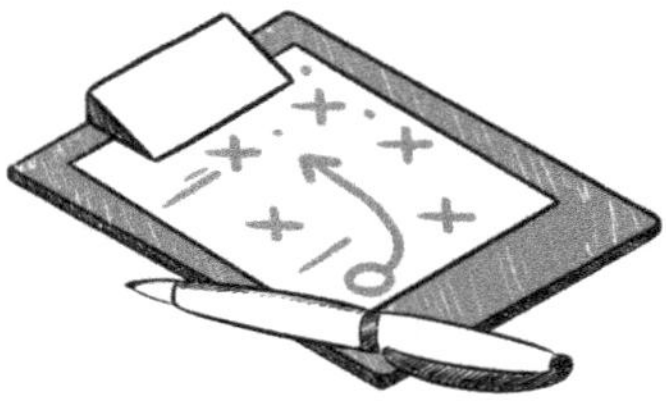

I mentioned earlier that many of my discussions with attorneys related to their approach to growth highlight tactics as opposed to strategies. It's no wonder why. If *Teams* are the *who*, Tactics are the *how* in executing your strategy.

Let's again distinguish between strategies and tactics.

A strategy refers to a long-term plan for achieving a particular goal or set of goals. It outlines the overarching approach to achieving the desired outcome and provides a roadmap for making progress towards it. A strategy is typically broader in scope and focuses on the big picture compared to tactics.

Tactics are the specific actions or methods used to execute that strategy. Tactics are more concrete and focused on the details of how to achieve the goals outlined in the strategy.

For example, if my weight loss strategy were to achieve a calorie deficit, implement a fitness regiment, and seek support, my tactics may include fasting until noon, participating in a daily spin class, and joining an online community.

Tactics get to the core of what the team will do to achieve the targets they have outlined.

Tactics will vary greatly by department and by target, and we will outline many of the tactics as we dissect each of the components of The Law Firm Growth Machine. Among those that will be familiar to you are marketing tactics like Search Engine Optimization, paid ads, or television commercials, whereas the intake team will need to employ specific call handling and conversion tactics like automated engagement messages and language that demonstrates empathy.

The pace at which tactics evolve is why strategy is so important to your firm's long-term success. Just looking back a decade ago, you will likely remember couldn't-fail tactics that, today, are fruitless. Marketing tactics in particular require a constant ear to the industry for what is driving success and what has grown stale. Keeping up with the changes in tactics, let alone how to execute them at a high level, is increasingly challenging.

That's why Tracking is more important than ever.

Tracking: Measuring Growth Performance

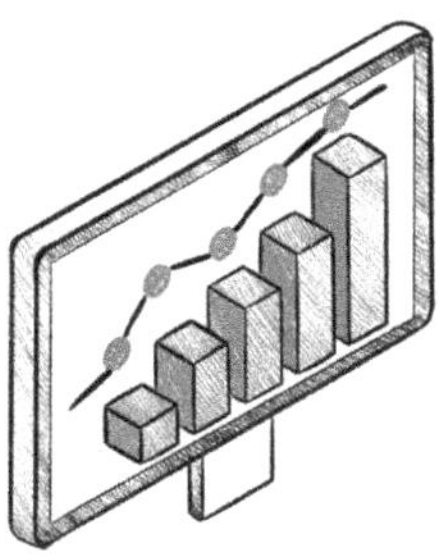

Your team needs to know what's working, what isn't, and why. To reference the old weight loss analogy again, that which is measured (daily/weekly weigh ins), is managed (continued progress).

Tracking performance, whether that's the number of calls received, leads screened, buttons clicked, or cases signed, is how you will inform the teams as to what tactics are working and which are not.

As a society, and as an industry, data is becoming increasingly important as we strain to beat the challenges we face in the market, and in an industry as competitive and costly as the legal industry, failing to track can mean failing to realize a positive return on investment.

As you seek to set your flywheel in motion, tracking progress toward those targets will provide invaluable insight into driving growth for your firm.

If you are just starting out, don't delay. Start tracking before you do anything else. You can't set reasonable targets if you don't know where you are, what you are currently achieving, or what you did to get there.

As we take a deeper look into each of the components of The Law Firm Growth Machine, we'll examine what should be tracked across your organization. The secret to your success just may be hidden in these figures!

Thankfully, tracking your firm data has never been easier, and that's because of the vast array of tools available to your teams.

Tools: Finding the Correct Fit

There is a right tool for every job, and surely this is true for a growth-minded law firm and the teams seeking to hit their targets.

Among the challenges law firms face is that there is such a wide choice of great tools from which to choose based on your needs, your practice areas, your size, and your goals.

As we have worked with clients over the years, we have found countless tools that support one's efforts to grow, but, again, these tools largely siloed their users.

Marketers may have found HubSpot met their needs while the intake team preferred Lead Docket for managing leads. Perhaps someone in the office was using Podium to enable texting and review management while another was scheduling social posts in Hootsuite.

Having each team working in separate tools makes it more difficult to collaborate toward that common goal - whatever that North Star Metric may be. Failing to communicate effectively across teams could actually inhibit growth as we have repeatedly cautioned.

For leadership seeking to overcome some of the many challenges in the industry, this lack of centralization makes it very difficult to track and measure performance or use that data to make decisions that improve outcomes.

Albert Einstein famously said: "Everything should be made as simple as possible, but not simpler." Law firms need to be selective in choosing tools that streamline workflows, save time, and increase effectiveness, but choosing from the vast array of options while keeping teams connected is one of the challenges we've often faced in light of the amazing solutions out there.

In the end, James and I decided we would have to build our own tool to break down the silos and still meet all the needs of the teams while prioritizing simplicity. What resulted was not only effective but this centralization of data provided invaluable insight that would help us make decisions that further drive growth.

We call it LOOP for its ability to close the loop between those all-important marketing, intake, and client service departments, provide essential feedback, and its ability to close the loop from lead to client and client to advocate that helps generate new leads.

Can you feel that flywheel spin?

LOOP is the system on which The Law Firm Growth Machine is built.

Closing Arguments

- In every strategy we employ and systemize, we must answer critical questions:
    - What are we trying to achieve?
    - Who will be responsible for overseeing each aspect of the process?
    - Who will be responsible for executing?
    - What tools will those individuals need to perform to the highest standard?
    - How will we hold people accountable?
    - How will we measure performance?
    - How will we communicate among those tasked with implementing the strategy?
- The Flywheel 5T, or F5T for short, is a framework to help firms answer these questions and identify the elements that will set their flywheel in motion.
- **The 5Ts are as follows:**
    - **Targets:** What is the goal that we are reaching toward?
    - **Team**: Who will execute, oversee, and be held accountable?
    - **Tactics**: What tactics will the team employ to achieve the goals?

- **Tracking**: How will we measure progress toward that goal?

- **Tools**: What tools will be required to reach these goals?

✲ To set the flywheel in motion, leadership must identify all 5Ts as they relate to marketing, intake, and client service.

"

The basics are the basics and they stay the basics.

KOBE BRYANT

CHAPTER 8

THE FUNDAMENTALS

Before we delve deeper into the mechanics of the growth machine, I want to recognize that there are core fundamentals that will have a profound effect on your firm's ability to successfully implement The Law Firm Growth Machine in your practice and achieve the success we have achieved with the clients with whom we have partnered. While we won't go into great depth on any of these four fundamentals, as entire books are dedicated to each subject, I do want to highlight their importance and suggest these subjects as foundational to the LFGM strategy.

They are:

1. A strong brand
2. The right people
3. Marketing investment
4. The CEO mindset

For just a moment, I want you to think of The Law Firm Growth Machine as a car.

You can liken the body of the car to your brand - shiny and new, stately and sophisticated, loud and splashy. The driver, in this case, you or a member/members of your team, operates the vehicle. The gas, in the form of marketing resources, fuels the car. As CEO, you inspect the vehicle, oversee the dashboard, and ensure you are in peak condition for optimal performance.

Let's examine each of these components.

A Strong Brand

Let's talk about brand. Effectively developed, a brand can do a lot of the heavy lifting typically required to earn a stranger's trust. It is the result of a consistent and concerted effort to speak directly and personally to a targeted audience in a way that conveys your mission and value promise.

Your brand (if memorable) makes people *feel* something, tapping into the emotional centers that compel decision-making.

Logically, consumers know that generic acetaminophen is likely every bit as effective as the name brand, Tylenol, but the emotional brain is catering to a sick child and a vulnerable mom is willing to pay twice as much for the promise of exceptional care for her little one.

That's the value of a brand.

Branding serves several important functions that help propel your firm's growth. Effective branding will make your firm more memorable, help develop client loyalty, convey how you differ from your competitors, and position your firm as you want your market to perceive you - whether that is warm and approachable, elite and exceptional, or anything in between.

Taking time to define your brand intentionally is invaluable to your practice. I like to say your brand will be "by design" or "by default," meaning, if you don't make the effort to define your brand – it **will** define itself, and not always in the way you want to present your firm to the world.

So, whether you are just starting out or you've been in practice for years, bringing together your partners and stakeholders for a brand exercise is an important step in growing your firm.

There's a perceived value that comes with buying on-brand that defies reason. It's why we pay up (significantly!) for Apple products, Nike shoes, and Tide detergent — there's a promise, a perceived value above and beyond the product itself, and law firms need to leverage that emotional connection with their audience just like any other organization.

While there are volumes of books and experts dedicated to brand development, commit to these basics to define and steadfastly maintain your brand to maximize growth strategy and system:

1. **Identify your target audience**. Who are you trying to reach? What are their needs, fears, interests, hopes, and priorities?

2. **Define your unique value proposition**. What sets your firm apart from the competition? What unique benefits or solutions do you offer?

3. **Establish your brand personality**. What is the tone and voice of your brand? Are you serious and professional, or approachable and lighthearted?

4. **Develop your messaging**. Your messaging should communicate your value proposition and personality to your target audience. This includes developing a tagline or mission statement that encapsulates your brand's essence.

5. **Create visual elements**. Visual elements, such as a logo, color palette, and font selection, are important components of brand identity. These elements should reflect your brand personality and values.

6. **Consistency**. Consistency is key to building a strong brand. All marketing and communication efforts should be aligned with your brand's identity and messaging.

Remember, brands don't happen overnight. Be consistent and deliberate with your branding and stick with it. Among the biggest mistakes we see firms make is that they don't actively market their brand to a broad audience, investing both time and money to broaden the reach of their firm, giving up too soon or investing too little.

It's worth noting that firms that win at attracting clients are not always the best firms (I know you find that infuriating!). Rather, they are the best *known* firms. We are all constantly surrounded by and consume a steady diet of media. Make sure you are part of that media by putting your firm in front of others with consistency and intention.

The Right People

When we study the F5T Framework, Team is a critical component of every system working to execute your strategy and oversee the systems. But, let's step away from the tactical things those members of the team are doing and look instead at the personalities and mindsets required if you are going to lead a growth-driven firm.

First, your efforts to grow your firm will be far more successful if your team is bought into the idea of growth, and that's not a given. If you are about to upset the apple cart by unveiling a new strategy, implementing new systems, imposing strict brand guidelines and the like, you may be met with some pushback. Change is scary, but the benefits of working for a growing firm versus a stagnant one are numerous and should be shared.

Typically, in a small practice, employees wear many hats, and if you are a solo practitioner, you're wearing them all! But, growing firms make it possible for individuals to specialize in and focus on areas where they excel.

Growth also generates stability and security for employees, and job security is important for one's emotional well-being. When your employees feel financially secure, they will be better able to serve clients and meet the demands of their roles, not to mention opportunities for increased salaries, bonuses, or career advancement.

All of the above make for a far better work environment than one in which business is slow, leadership is stressed, budgets are tight, and morale is low. The business performs better when clients are motivated and engaged, and employees are motivated and engaged when the business performs well. It's a chicken-and-egg relationship that benefits everyone.

So, fire up your troops! This is exciting!

With your Law Firm Growth Machine strategy and systems implemented, you will also find your team is better able to spend their time on meaningful tasks that help create advocates of clients. Automating manual tasks is a core component of The Law Firm Growth Machine, and that means your team will save considerable time. Time that is best spent serving clients.

That is what will differentiate your firm from others and make the flywheel spin, so your team simply must adopt a client-centered mindset.

What is a client-centered mindset? A client-centered mindset means prioritizing the needs and interests of the client in all aspects of the firm's operations, from the initial consultation to the final outcome of the case.

This is achieved by practicing active listening, building rapport with the caller, being transparent, communicating regularly and personally, and acting with compassion and empathy.

If your firm is going to set the flywheel in motion, this absolutely must be the default in how you deliver service. The challenge is that when we live in this space for so long, we too often become desensitized to the realities of what clients are telling us.

When we fail to recognize the humanity of our clients and the crisis they are facing in the moment they reach out to us, we overlook an opportunity to build a relationship and play the hero. Heroes win referrals.

In addition to being empathetic and client-centered, your team will also need to be goals-oriented and data-driven.

The Law Firm Growth Machine is designed to help firms make decisions that drive growth, and that requires that your people share your commitment to identifying targets, tracking data, and reporting results. This is beneficial for growth, of course, but also for your culture, team cohesiveness, employee morale, and productivity.

Marketing Investment

According to a survey conducted by the American Bar Association in 2020, 43% of lawyers reported that acquiring new clients was a major challenge for their practice with another 30% saying it was a significant challenge. For solo and small firms, those numbers were even higher (which is why James and I made a rally cry of the mantra "Leave no lead behind!").

Of course, to capture that lead and retain the client, you have to first get the click or call.

But, how?

Marketing is fundamental to a law firm's growth strategy. If you don't intend to invest in growth through marketing efforts, your firm will struggle to compete in a saturated market.

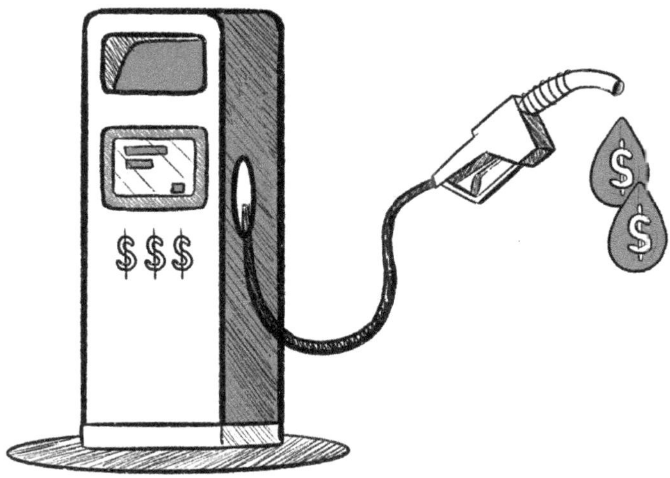

Marketing is the fuel in your growth machine.

In 2014, almost a decade ago mind you, Lawyernomics, a division of AVVO, found that 96% of consumers begin their search for an attorney online. You can imagine in the nine years since, that number has only grown. Therefore, practices must invest in online marketing. Given current market conditions, this is indeed costly - but as I've said before, and I'll say again, marketing is not an expense - it's an investment.

Until more recently with the advent of some new Google solutions, online marketing required skills that are not present in every law firm. While a vast network of "experts" offer online marketing services, it's difficult to tell who's good and who's not without investing significantly, which can prove particularly costly if the efforts don't pay off.

With the advent of Google's Local Service Ads for lawyers, even solo practices can now advertise online with minimal risk. LSAs, as they are commonly known, can be effective, affordable (especially if you have an optimized intake system like The Law Firm Growth Machine), and easy to implement.

Paid traffic to your website, search engine optimization, lead generation services, and pay-per-call/click are just a few of the options available to firms seeking online marketing solutions and tactics that we have seen successfully (and unsuccessfully) employed by many of the firms we have worked with.

I also strongly recommend a budget to cultivate relationships with your legal community and referral sources. As you invest in marketing, you must budget, track it, and, above all, measure the return on that investment, which we will discuss in greater detail shortly.

The bottom line is this: you have to spend money to make money, and, generally, those who spend more make more.

A 2018 joint study between Bloomberg Law and the Legal Marketing Association found that the average law firm invested about 7% of its gross revenue on marketing while high-growth firms, according to Hinge Marketing, dedicated 27% of their revenue - 48% more than low-growth firms.

As you'll recall from our brief discussion on brand, often, the most successful firms aren't the best but simply the best known. If you are a great firm, your marketing efforts will pay off even more as you effectively communicate your expertise and value to your target audience and reap the benefits of satisfied clients referring your practice to those who will already be familiar with your brand and are that much more likely to retain your services.

Marketing in the legal industry has a storied past from those early days of the post Arizona v. Bates era, and the environment in the time since is unrecognizable. As our world has changed, so must our approach to generating business. Marketing - especially online - is simply fundamental to your firm's success.

The CEO Mindset

The use of the title CEO is becoming more common in the halls of law offices, and not necessarily by a managing partner. Historically, law firms were managed by lawyers with little emphasis on business strategy or management practices. However, as the industry has become more competitive and complex, many law firms have recognized the need for professional management expertise to drive growth and profitability.

As laws continue to evolve and even allow for non-lawyer partnership in firms, as has become the case in Arizona, Utah, and Washington, D.C., this is likely to become only more common.

The role of the CEO in a law practice is to bring a business-focused perspective to the management of the firm and to develop and implement strategic plans to achieve growth and profitability. As CEO, you may be responsible for managing financial resources, human resources, and other key operational functions, such as marketing, business development, and client acquisition.

As you embark on your growth journey, you will need to approach opportunities and challenges from this perspective by embracing these statements:

I drive the strategic vision for this firm.

This is your firm, and you need to define what you want it to be and rally those around you to bring it to fruition. To do so, you must articulate this vision, and provide the necessary resources to make it a reality. Build a team that shares the vision, empower them to execute, and hold them accountable.

I am goal-oriented, data-driven, and focused on continuous improvement.

Jim Barksdale said, "If we have data, let's look at the data. If all we have are opinions, let's go with mine." Among the many benefits of creating systems (not to mention simply living in a digital world) is that we are creating and collecting countless data points that can inform the decision-making that drives growth. As CEO, commit to centralizing, visualizing, and analyzing the data to achieve your goals. Begin with knowing the numbers fundamental to growth and put data in the driver's seat.

I foster a client-centered culture and lead my team in a way that enables them to provide this level of high-quality care and service.

Success in a service industry, and especially with the LFGM strategy in play, requires a steadfast commitment to putting the client experience first. As the CEO of your law firm, it is critical that you foster an environment that makes it possible for your team to deliver this service. This means prioritizing active listening, building strong relationships, and acting with compassion and empathy in all interactions with clients. A client-centered mindset not only helps to build strong relationships with your clients that will drive additional opportunity for the firm, but it will help your firm stand out among your competition.

I break down silos between departments to achieve better outcomes.

Lack of collaboration across departments is one of the greatest detriments to growth. As CEO, you must facilitate collaboration and create feedback loops that drive the firm toward its goals. This requires a commitment to open communication, a willingness to listen to ideas and feedback from all members of your team, and a focus on creating a culture of teamwork and shared success.

I am in tune and informed with regard to my market, the industry, and the broader business community.

As CEO, you are the face of your organization, and you need presence in your community not only to bring attention to your firm but also to build awareness of market conditions, business opportunities, referral and networking relationships, and emerging trends. Lawyers have lived too long in a lawyers-only club, and, as noted with changes to ownership structures especially, the space is poised for change. As CEO, you are tasked with not only staying abreast of changes and influences, but proactively positioning your firm for continued success.

Closing Arguments

Before implementing the LFGM strategy in your practice, ensure that you have a solid foundation for growth by assessing your commitment to the four fundamentals of law firm growth:

- **A Strong Brand**

  Effective branding can make your firm more memorable, develop client loyalty, and position your firm as you want your market to perceive you. Your brand is the result of a consistent and concerted effort to speak directly and personally to a targeted audience in a way that conveys your mission and value promise. Remember that brands don't happen overnight and require active marketing to a broad audience.

- **The Right People**

  By adopting a client-centered mindset and hiring individuals who embrace this approach, your team can prioritize clients' needs and interests, build relationships, and win referrals. Additionally, being goals-oriented and data-driven can help your team make decisions that drive growth, improve team cohesiveness, and increase productivity.

- **Marketing Investment**

  Acquiring new clients is a challenge for lawyers and law firms, particularly for solo and small firms. Marketing is essential in growing your practice as it is the fuel of your growth machine. With 96% of consumers beginning their search for an attorney online, online marketing has become increasingly important, but given the high costs of marketing, firms need to budget, track, and measure their return on investment.

✲ The CEO Mindset

Many lawyers are unprepared by their training to operate and grow a business, but by adopting the CEO mindset, lawyers can increase their aptitude for growth, profitability, and long-term success, all of which are increasingly important as the industry becomes more competitive. As the CEO of your law firm, you must embrace these concepts:

- I drive the strategic vision for this firm.
- I am goal-oriented, data-driven, and focused on continuous improvement.
- I foster a client-centered culture and lead my team in a way that enables them to provide this level of high-quality care and service.
- I break down silos between departments to achieve better outcomes.
- I am in tune and informed with regard to my market, the industry, and the broader business community.

PART THREE

How to Build Your Machine

A WORD FROM JAMES

Before jumping into Part 3, it's important to mention The Fourth Industrial Revolution, or Industry 4.0, which is a term used to describe the current trend of automation and data exchange in just about every industry, including legal.

Law firms that embrace Industry 4.0 will be well-positioned to grow their practices and succeed in an increasingly competitive legal marketplace. Legal tech tools can automate routine tasks and enable law firms to offer new services, while data analytics can provide insights into clients' industries and legal trends.

In Part 2 of the book, Kerri provided a step-by-step guide to creating a growth strategy that can transform your law firm. Now, in part 3, she shows you how to capitalize on Industry 4.0 by systemizing that strategy and leveraging data. She takes you behind the scenes and reveals the tools and systems our team has built so you can build your own growth machine, or plug into ours.

First up is the Client Retention Engine. This turnkey intake system leverages automation, intelligent workflows and call tracking to turn more of these leads into retained cases. It was responsible for generating over $14 million in case value for one client alone last year. You get to see the exact steps involved in building this system, so you can implement it in your own law firm.

Next is the Client Satisfaction Sensor. It's a fully automated system that looks to engage your clients for feedback. We measure this using a metric called the Net Promoter Score (NPS). Generating this feedback from your clients enables your firm to tackle issues quickly and prevent them from manifesting. It is a powerful way of minimizing, and even eliminating those reputation-crushing 1-star reviews online.

The final system covered by Kerri is the Client Advocate Amplifier, which leverages AI. This end-to-end system will help you generate, respond to, and even share reviews on social media... on autopilot! Imagine having five-star reviews feed in consistently for your law firm, without really having to lift a finger. This is a fascinating glimpse into the world of AI and Kerri provides all the details you need to build such a powerful system for your firm.

Finally, Kerri refers to The Pulse, a central hub where law firms can track their growth KPIs. This system allows you to monitor your law firm's progress in real-time, so you can make better-informed growth decisions. Kerri makes a strong case for KPIs and data analytics in this section, explaining why they're critical to the success of any law firm growth strategy. She gives you a list of the KPIs she tracks for her clients and what it takes to build your own.

Part 3 of The Law Firm Growth Machine book is a must-read for any law firm looking to systemize their growth.

"

The engine
is the heart
of an airplane,
but the pilot
is its soul.

WALTER RALEIGH

CHAPTER 9

THE CLIENT RETENTION ENGINE

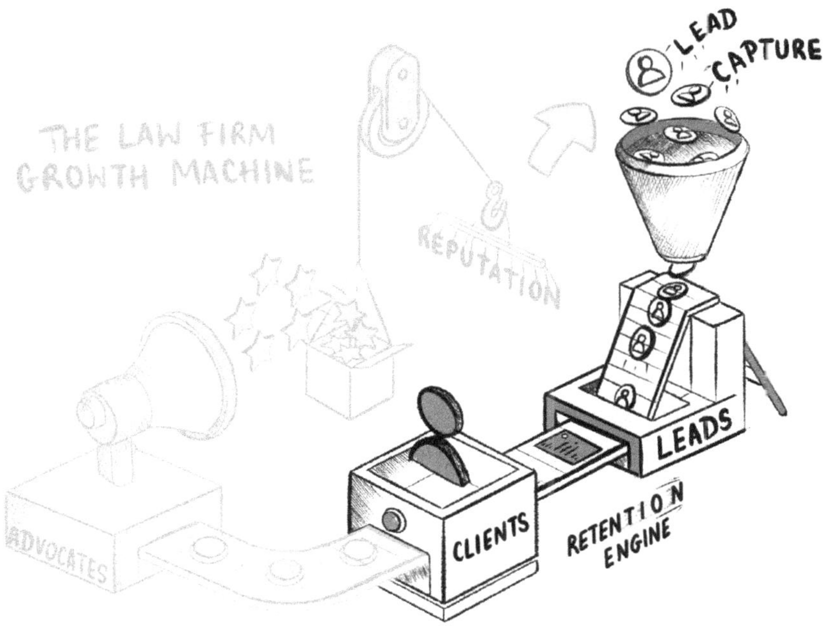

Let's revisit the idea of your growth machine as a car. You have the body, the operator and fuel, but it's time to look under the hood to where the real work of moving forward is done: The engine.

The engine in your growth machine is the client retention engine. This is the mechanism for capturing leads and effectively converting those leads into clients.

In the pages that follow we will explore how best to maximize lead capture and conversion.

Before we delve deeper into the processes of capturing and converting leads though, let's first take a quick look at the core elements of The Client Retention Engine.

Inside the Engine: Get to know the parts

To discuss the Client Retention Engine we must first align our language. I'll be talking about the four parts of the engine as follows:

The Lead Form: Paramount to signing more clients is streamlining all lead activity. This means that every lead whether it is a call to the office, an email from a former client, a handwritten note from a referral partner, or contact details submitted via your website is entered into your system. Ideally, some leads will enter your system through direct integrations while others will need to be manually added to the form. In the KerriJames Law Firm Growth Machine, leads entered into the lead form are immediately pushed into the firm's pipeline for lead management as well as the marketing contact list.

The Pipeline: The lead journey is best illustrated in a pipeline. The pipeline is where all leads from your lead form land. Converting a client is a sales process. You are selling your firm's ability to solve the prospect's problem. Each stage of the pipeline from New Lead to Retained Client requires different strategies and has unique goals to help move the prospect through to the next stage.

The Campaigns: A campaign is an organized course of action to achieve a goal, and as noted, each stage of the pipeline will have a different goal. Therefore, campaign messages delivered by your team on calls, in emails, voicemails, or text messages at each stage of the pipeline, are designed to move the prospect closer to retaining your services.

The Human Element: We've consistently emphasized the importance of the right people on the job and in no role is it more important than as operator of your client retention engine. The individual operating the engine needs to understand the prospect's needs, the messaging contained in the campaigns, the goals at each stage of the pipeline, your firm's expertise, and the tools he or she has available to retain the client. And of course, this all needs to be executed with an empathetic, client-centered approach in a very timely manner.

Before we move on, let's also define leads.

A lead is a prospective client who has shown interest in your services. This is an invitation to provide value, highlight your expertise, and build a relationship in which he or she may come to know, like, and trust you.

At KerriJames, we classify leads as a call lead (someone who contacts the office by phone) or an e-lead (someone for whom we have received contact information - typically via electronic submission).

Call leads represent your highest-intent prospects. These are the individuals whose information can be entered into the lead form most comprehensively as they speak to your team. E-leads are those leads for whom you have received contact details but they have not yet called the office. They may come in the form of online lead gen, form fills/chats/surveys/opt-ins on your website, online leads from social media and your Google Business Profile, or leads delivered from sources like SuperLawyers, AVVO or even referral partners delivered to your email inbox.

Ideally, an e-lead would automatically enter into your intake system through a direct integration between the lead source (such as your website) and your intake system (for example, Lawmatics, Lead Docket or LOOP, the software on which we built The Law Firm Growth Machine). This means you do not have to re-enter the information the lead has provided into the lead form - it's already in your intake system.

All others - calls, non-integrated e-leads, those leads delivered via email from lead sources like referral partners - should be entered into the lead form with the intention that you will collect additional information once you get the prospect on a call.

Now that you understand the parts of The Client Retention Engine, let's take a look at how we capture and convert clients to grow your firm.

Lead Capture: Transforming Attention into Opportunity

With a glowing reputation generating increased awareness of your firm, you'll want to ensure that every potential lead is captured.

You'll recall that the marketing team is tasked with generating leads for your firm and may utilize tactics such as SEO (Search Engine Optimization) to drive traffic to your website.

With nearly 100% of those seeking legal advice turning first to the internet, including those who are referred, it's well advised to have tools in place to capture as many of those site visitors as possible.

While this may sound obvious, it's more nuanced than ever with an entire generation of individuals whose preference is to communicate without ever picking up the phone.

When I meet with a prospective client seeking to improve client retention, I first look for "the low-hanging fruit" - the quick, easy wins that can produce results without a ton of resources or effort. In a law firm, that low-hanging fruit is typically the result of a few changes to the website to capture more leads.

Capture More Leads on your Website

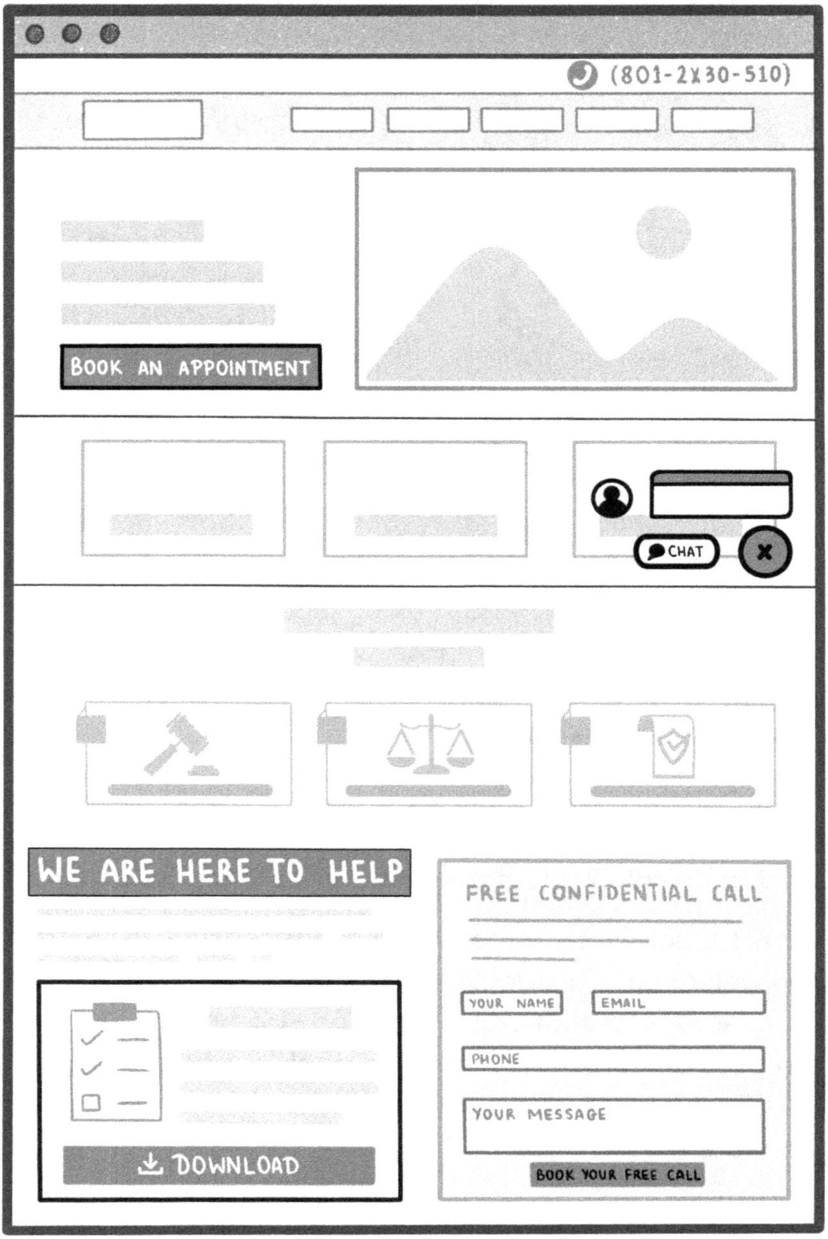

Let's take a look at the six conversion points your website should offer to turn it from an online brochure into a lead-generating machine:

1. Tracked phone numbers

It goes without saying that your phone number should be large and easy to find on your website. These numbers can actually connect directly to your intake system so that every call is tracked and recorded to improve your ability to identify lead sources and as well as provide material for internal training.

2. Form Fill

Most firms have some sort of contact form on their website, but does yours simply create an email or does it direct prospective clients into your pipeline where they are quickly engaged?

Your contact form should follow some basic logic based on the user's selections.

In addition to contact information and comments, add a drop-down labeled "How can we help?" with the following options:

- I am an existing client.
- I may need a lawyer.
- Something else.

Based on the selection, leads (I may need a lawyer) can be directed into the intake pipeline where they are immediately engaged with a message that lets them know we are reviewing their inquiry and will follow up with them shortly.

Notice that I added the word 'may,' as opposed to the more decisive "I need a lawyer." This subtle language tweak invites those who aren't ready to hire an attorney, but who you now have the opportunity to nurture through your pipeline.

3. Self-Serve Options (surveys, calculators, etc)

Your website should engage users in a meaningful way with self-serve options such as a calculator or survey. This supports your SEO efforts and acts as a lead generator.

Examples of a survey that prospects can use on your site include "Do I have a case?" "What's my case worth," or something similarly suited to your practice area. The user provides their contact details to acquire their "results."

4. Booking Widget

Among the most effective conversion tools we have implemented for our growth-minded clients is a scheduling widget on their website.

With so many attorneys offering free consultations, a booking widget makes tremendous sense. These tools integrate with your existing calendar, can be customized for specific availability, rotate among staff, and remind the prospect of their upcoming appointment.

For our clients, these scheduled consultations are some of the most high-intent prospects. Tools like Appointment Thing, Calendly, and Acuity can sync with your personal and business calendar, send reminders, and provide booking structures to control access.

5. Chatbots

Millennials and Gen Z in particular are more inclined to engage with a chatbot than to place a call. A study by Harris Poll on behalf of Salesforce, found that 69% of millennials prefer chat to phone when engaging with businesses, including law firms. Yet according to the ABA's 2021 survey, live chat was offered on only 6% of respondents' websites.

There are three types of chatbots to consider:

- Traditional chatbot that can roll over to live chat
- AI-chatbot that's based on a significant knowledge base
- Text chatbot that rolls over to the prospect's mobile messaging app

Chatbots can take the first step in engaging a prospect on your website, encouraging the site visitor to take action. This engagement can also improve your site's ranking as time on page is a factor in search engine optimization.

Of course, the chatbot is doing the work for you when your practice is closed, providing assistance at any time of day or night, even outside of normal business hours. In an increasingly "on-demand" society, this can be a competitive advantage if your competitors hold to traditional business hours.

Our clients have signed many of their own clients who connected with the firm initially over chat. In fact, last year, one client with whom we utilize a combination AI-chatbot that rolls over to a live agent, generated 539 opportunities via chat alone!

6. Lead Magnet

If you don't have a lead magnet providing value to your prospective clients before they engage you, this is another excellent option. Offering free resources or content in exchange for a potential client's contact information is not only a way to feed your pipeline, but it's also an excellent way to showcase your expertise, showcase your brand, and throw in some social proof. Consider a checklist, an e-book, or a planning document.

Additional Lead Capture Strategies

It goes without saying that if you want to capture leads while your competition sleeps, call centers specifically trained to handle legal prospects can ensure that the middle-of-the-night call is not missed. Flexible pricing plans through companies like Smith.ai make such services affordable for even the smallest firms. But, the reality is that even call centers can miss a call.

In this case, the missed-called message is brilliant and personal.

This is a feature we've built into The Law Firm Growth Machine that not only saves leads that may otherwise call another attorney if your firm doesn't answer, but actually shows a personal touch that can be a real differentiator.

Here's how it works:

When a call from a new number is missed, the caller receives a message such as the following:

> *Hi, it's Kyle Smith, the attorney you were just trying to reach. So sorry I couldn't grab the call just then. I'll ring back in just a few!*

Call centers remain your safest bet to ensure no call is missed.

Capturing Leads through Social Media

Lastly, don't overlook leads that communicate with your firm through social media! Social Media is used by more than half the world's population and Americans in particular are spending about half their time on their phone on these platforms. It's incredibly important that your firm is responding to leads in a timely manner by pushing these leads into your pipeline too.

As you build your law firm growth machine, you'll want to ensure that you are able to connect directly with Google, Facebook, Instagram, and TikTok so that any communication through these channels isn't overlooked.

Optimizing your lead capture capabilities with these tactics will surely result in additional opportunities for your firm. But again, leads aren't clients! So let's get to converting them!

Conversion: The Lead-to-Client Journey

Conversion from lead to client is the work of your intake team. If your intake team is operating much as they did ten or even five years ago - you have fallen behind - behind the times, behind the expectations of today's empowered (and vocal!) consumers, and quite possibly behind your competition.

The conversion system built into The Client Retention Engine is designed to convert more leads to clients with greater efficiency and far less effort, squeezing every last drop of juice out of your marketing budget.

Pipeline Stages & Campaigns: Management & Messaging

The Pipeline reflects the Lead-to-Client Journey. Let's explore each step in the pipeline and how you can increase your conversions with effective campaign messaging.

Stage 1: New Lead

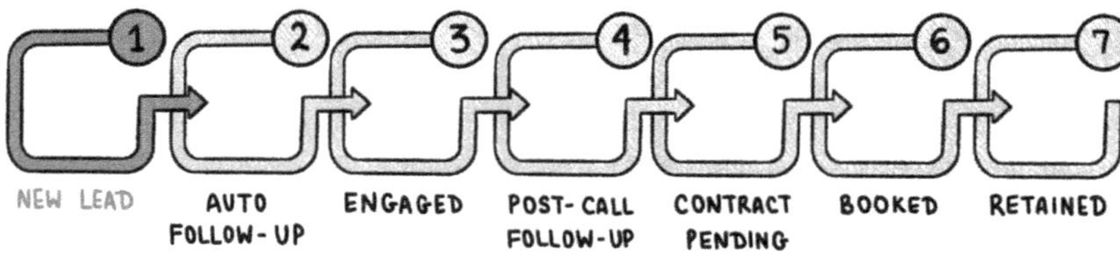

Every lead that comes in as information instead of direct outreach over the phone is a new lead. You can think of this as a "warm lead." The individual may have raised their hand to say they are interested in your services, opted-in to a lead magnet on your website, submitted a form, or been referred to you by another attorney.

The goal with every New Lead is to get the individual to engage personally by letting you know they are ready to talk.

Quickly contacting the lead by phone is the intake tactic most apt to result in a new client. So in addition to sending the prospect an immediate engagement message, you'll also want to inform the team that there is a new lead and that someone must quickly place a call.

Enter all New Leads into the lead form. In addition to populating the pipeline, you are building your list of future clients for marketing purposes. That's why every lead (not just the "good" ones) should be entered.

LOOP, the software on which we custom built The Law Firm Growth Machine, integrates directly with Facebook, Instagram, Google Business Profiles and TikTok so that any messages within those platforms are automatically entered into the pipeline in the New Lead stage. Custom integrations from your website, lead providers, chat services and more can further streamline your lead management.

The campaign used at this stage of the pipeline is the auto-engagement message followed by an outbound call to the prospect as quickly as possible.

Stage 2: Auto-Follow-Up

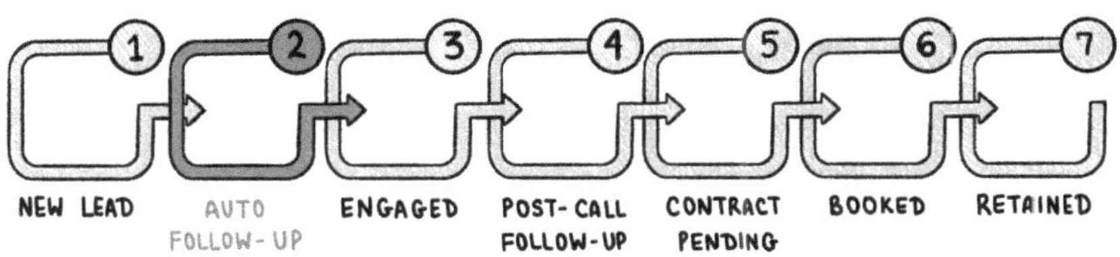

The best outreach for a hot lead will always be a call, but if you are not successful in getting the prospect on the phone, the intake professional should drop the lead into the Auto-Follow-Up stage of the pipeline. It is here that the prospect is entered into the Auto-Follow-Up Campaign. This campaign is designed to engage the caller, prompting him or her to let us know a good time to talk, to book a consultation, or otherwise tell us how we can help.

A consistent follow-up system is imperative, but challenging to execute manually. We're all very busy, and the reality is that a lot of messages will be ignored until a convenient time. But, we have a certain responsibility to help those we can. An automated follow-up system will ensure that every prospect is given every opportunity to engage with you until they either say they are ready or they prefer not to engage.

The winning follow-up campaign built into The Law Firm Growth Machine is one in which every lead is contacted by phone daily until they are Engaged, inform the firm they are not interested, or reach the end of the campaign, while automated text messages and emails encourage the prospect to respond with a date and time they are able to connect personally.

As you build your growth system, outline the precise campaign every prospect will enter to maximize conversions.

Stage 3: Engaged

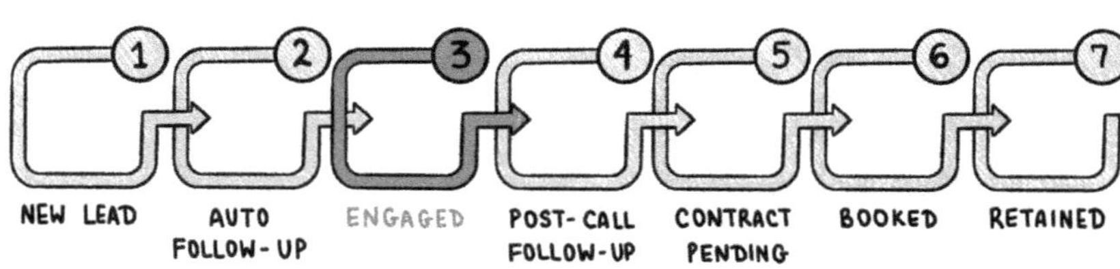

A lead who is interacting with your firm is an Engaged Lead. This typically comes in the form of a call to the office or a response to the auto-follow-up campaign. This is as hot as a lead gets and when your team needs to respond with speed, empathy, authority, and leadership.

If the lead is engaged via text or email, the goal is to get the prospect on a call or booked for a consultation. If the contact is already engaged by phone, the goal is to get the client to sign a simple engagement letter or schedule an appointment to do so (subject to the firm's process).

If your firm misses the call (the horror!), the lead is a New Lead (not an engaged lead) though they would receive (and hopefully respond to) the missed-call text back.

If the firm is able to help the client, KerriJames encourages electronic delivery of a simple engagement letter that can be executed via email while supporting the client over the phone. You can use the time between signing and the full intake to share a welcome video that highlights the firm's successes and prepares the client for the next step in their journey.

Stage 4: Post-Call Follow-Up

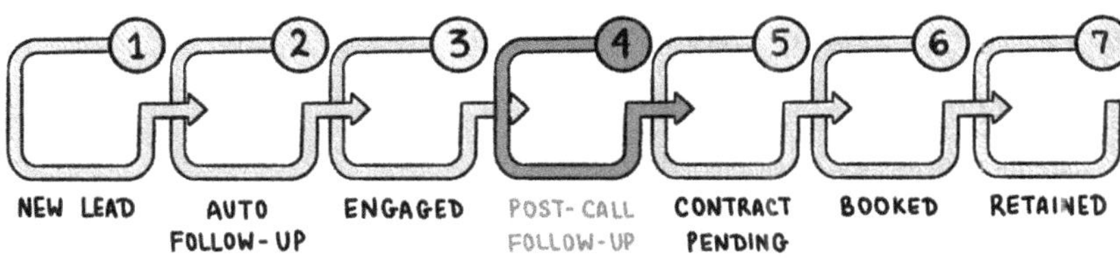

Not every lead is ready for the one-call close. Some will need to discuss their steps with a spouse, may want to look up your reviews, or otherwise take some time to consider their options. That's why a post-call follow-up is important.

Following a phone call with an undecided prospect that we are in fact able to help, the intake professional moves the lead into "Post Call Follow-Up." In this campaign, the prospect is first thanked for their time on the phone and provided with the contact details they will need to reach out again when they are ready. A series of emails and text messages add value, provide social proof of your firm's successes such as 5-star reviews, testimonials, or case studies, and offer support.

Stage 5: Contract Pending

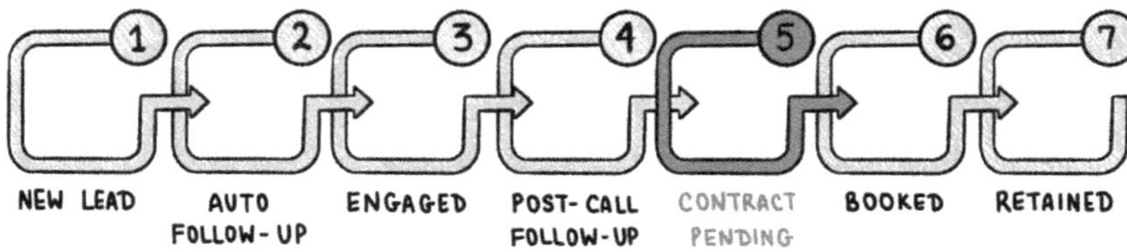

When an Engaged client is ready to sign an engagement letter, having an electronic document delivery service can reduce friction and increase conversions.

We have found the greatest signing success when the firm electronically delivers a simple engagement letter as opposed to an overly comprehensive intake document. When you have effectively sold your firm to the prospect, you need to capture that signature. We recommend a one-page engagement agreement as a first step, followed by a scheduled intake.

Breaking this step into two also allows your new client to enjoy the moment of burden transfer, gather whatever documents they may need to complete the thorough intake, and set aside an appropriate amount of time, free from distraction.

This time-lapse provides yet another opportunity for the new client to review the accolades and results they may not have seen if they hadn't been through a follow-up campaign. It's a way to further highlight your expertise and showcase your attentive client care.

If the prospect doesn't sign while on the phone, don't worry. There's a campaign for that too! If your client is sitting in Contract Pending, then your team knows they are working toward a signature. These visual cues make lead management all the easier.

The Contract Pending campaign begins with thanking the caller for their time and letting them know that, as promised, the document was delivered to their email inbox. This campaign sequence is delivered only via text message as most electronic delivery systems will have an email follow up sequence built in.

Note again that these messages are designed to elicit a response and let the prospect know we are here to help. Messaging typically asks questions like, "Did you have any questions about the engagement letter I sent over?" "Can I answer any additional questions for you?" and "Would you like to walk through the document together?"

Stage 6: Booked

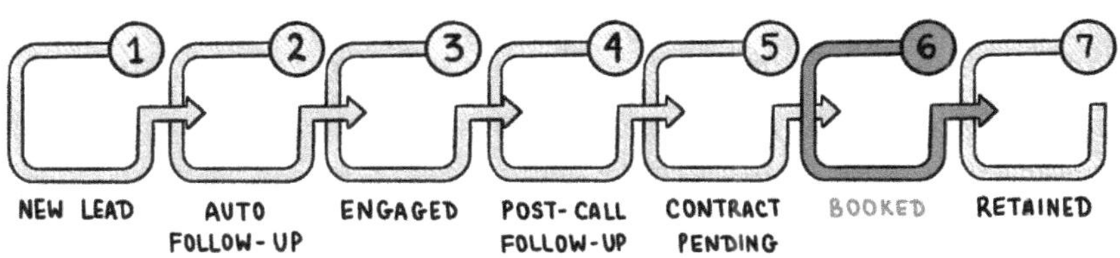

A client lives in the "Booked" stage, which can also be referenced in your pipeline as "Intake" or "Onboarding" until such time that the full intake is complete. Your intake or onboarding should have a thorough process in and of itself.

In addition to collecting all the necessary information required to complete the intake, you should have a means for communicating exactly what clients can expect throughout their engagement, how best to communicate with your firm, and what the very next step will be.

Providing the client with written materials or a high-quality video is well-advised here.

Communication in this stage begins with confirmation of the booked appointment and details as to what he or she will need to do or bring to prepare for the meeting.

Stage 7: Retained

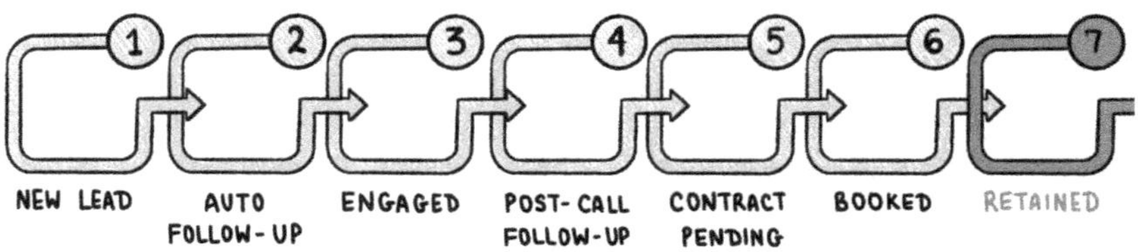

At this stage of the lead-to-client journey you have completed all necessary agreements, gathered documentation, and begun to build the client file. Moving a lead to this stage is the end of their lead journey, but the beginning of their client journey. Mindful that intake is a sales role, this is when the client is officially marked WON (ring the bell!).

At this stage, your communications should include an official welcome from the firm. This can come in the form of a video, a snail-mail welcome packet to the home, or even a bit of firm "swag."

This is a great opportunity to stand out as a personal, client-centered, eager-to-please firm.

This is also an excellent time to request feedback regarding the client's intake experience. Constantly improving your intake experience should be a priority in your practice. Request feedback and learn from it.

Once marked won indicating the client has been retained, the lead syncs to a new pipeline in which the client service team takes over. And so begins the efforts to keep the client satisfied.

A final word about The Client Retention Engine

If this feels like a lot to take in let alone implement, you're right. It is. Heck! It was a lot for us just to write out the process! But, believe me when I tell you this – no other system will affect your bottom line more than one to capture and convert leads.

The right client retention engine will enable your firm to operate at an incredibly high level whether you are solo, small, or established but leaking leads. This is a classic case of slowing down to accelerate. Do it.

And if you can't, we can help. We've codified years of knowledge and built a plug-n-play system based on data from our custom engagements to effectively convert legal prospects into high-value clients regardless of your size.

Closing Arguments

- An effective client retention engine is at the heart of a growth system and serves one very clear purpose: capture and convert leads!

- The key elements of The Client Retention Engine are the lead form, the pipeline, high-converting campaigns, and empathetic operators.

- A powerful, effective and efficient client retention engine can significantly improve marketing return on investment while eliminating overwhelm on the staff.

- To capture more leads on your website firms should consider:
    - Call tracking numbers
    - Smart form fill
    - Self-serve options like a survey or calculator
    - A booking widget
    - A chatbot
    - Lead Magnet

- Integrating your intake system with lead sources such as social media platforms, lead gen providers, and Google can ensure no lead is left behind while text back features and call centers can prevent the loss of opportunities that may otherwise be missed.

✲ An optimized conversion system should:

- Ensure every lead is immediately engaged, even when you miss a call.
- Centralize leads for easy management using an opportunity pipeline.
- Deliver personal follow up messages and campaigns to move the lead through the pipeline.
- Effortlessly deliver retainers and request signatures.
- Schedule appointments and send text reminders, directions, and relevant reminders to ensure prospects show up.
- Follow up with any prospect who fails to make it to an appointment.
- Solicit feedback regarding the intake experience.

"

Feedback is the breakfast of champions.

KEN BLANCHARD

CHAPTER 10

THE CLIENT SATISFACTION SENSOR

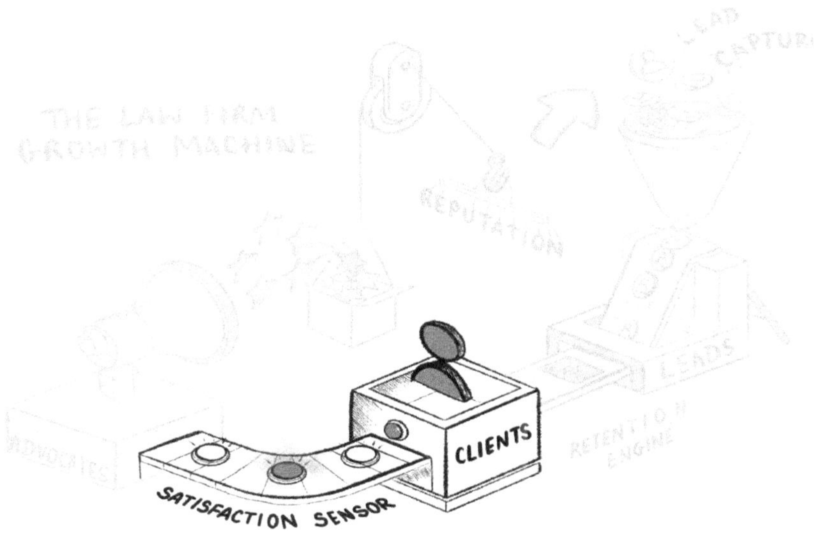

Your client retention engine may be driving growth, but any good machine is going to have sensors that continuously assess the system. You may be familiar with an alarm going off if your engine is running hot or your tires need air and that helps ensure that your vehicle is in good health.

Similarly, you want to ensure that critical functions in your practice are at peak performance.

If you are going to generate the flywheel effect in your business, you are going to have to elevate clients to advocates. That requires maintaining their satisfaction throughout their engagement.

So let's take a look at the Client Satisfaction Sensor, the ongoing monitoring system built into your growth machine.

Like the intake pipeline, having a client service pipeline provides a visual element to management that will prove helpful as you grow.

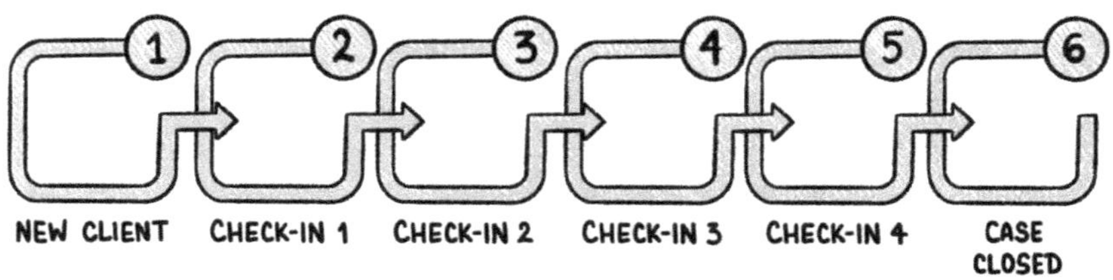

The stages of your pipeline may vary based on the practice area and typical length of an engagement, but all will begin at the New Client stage in which we solicit feedback regarding the intake experience using a measurement called the NPS or Net Promoter Score.

The Net Promoter Score is a client satisfaction metric that is used to assess how likely clients are to recommend your firm to others. As a brand new client, we make this first request following the intake experience and quarterly throughout the engagement.

Here's how that works for one of our personal injury clients:

1. Once the lead is moved to retained in the New Lead Pipeline, the team is notified of a new client which informs a team member to mail the firm's unique welcome (yours may be email, video, swag, etc. Differentiate yourself!).

2. The lead is marked "won" and syncs to the New Client Pipeline in the "New Client" stage.

3. Once in the New Client Pipeline, the first NPS messages are sent requesting feedback on the intake experience. The client is asked just one question:

   "On a scale of 0 to 10, how likely are you to recommend our firm to a friend or colleague?"

4. Every 90 days thereafter, the client automatically moves to the next stage of the pipeline triggering the NPS campaign.

5. If the client leaves a low score, a member of the team is notified to contact the client personally.

Calculating the NPS

By clicking a single button, clients assign a score to their answer ranging from one (not at all likely) to 10 (extremely likely). Respondents are then categorized into three groups based on their responses:

Promoters (9-10): These are customers who are highly satisfied with the product or service and are likely to recommend it to others.

Passives (7-8): These are customers who are satisfied but not particularly enthusiastic about the product or service. They may be more likely to switch to a competitor if a better option becomes available.

Detractors (0-6): These are customers who are dissatisfied with the product or service and are unlikely to recommend it to others.

To calculate the NPS score, subtract the percentage of detractors from the percentage of promoters. The resulting score can range from -100 to 100, with higher scores indicating higher customer satisfaction and a greater likelihood of customer loyalty and advocacy.

For example, consider a firm that has collected 50 NPS scores. Thirty-two of these are Promoters (64%), ten are passives (20%) and eight are detractors (16%). The NPS score is therefore 64 minus 16, which equals 48.

Is this a good NPS score?

Well, the creators of the NPS metric, Bain & Company, say yes. By their reckoning, an NPS score above 0 is good, above 20 is great and above 50 is amazing. Anywhere above 80 is the top percentile.

However, analyzing the absolute score alone is not enough. You must track the trend in score over time to ensure client satisfaction standards are maintained.

Utilizing NPS in Your Practice

NPS is a key performance indicator (KPI) for your practice and it can provide valuable insights into areas where improvements can be made, and specifically when to enhance the client experience. Based on scores you may learn when confidence wanes, when clients require increased communication, and when to intervene personally.

At the individual level, a low NPS score should notify the client service team that they should intervene personally. Often clients want only to voice their frustrations. This can help prevent the client from sharing negative feedback publicly or, even worse, losing the client to another firm.

Clients know that negative feedback shared publicly often motivates business owners to take action. But taking action before negative feedback makes its way into the public sphere is a far better way to conduct business and protect your reputation.

That's why it's imperative that firms routinely assess client satisfaction and intervene before it's too late, protecting not only the client relationship at hand but the firm's reputation at large.

Also of note, while it is against Google policy to reward clients for reviews, an NPS score is an internal metric that can be incentivized, which will often increase the number of participants and therefore the validity of the aggregate data.

Here's why we built the NPS campaign built into The Law Firm Growth Machine and why you should do the same for your growth system:

1. Avoid harsh public feedback: As we've discussed, negativity biases make it such that clients are more likely to leave negative feedback. Identify when client confidence starts deteriorating and make adjustments to your service delivery to avoid further decline. Reach out personally to clients who have negative feedback and let them share personally - they'll be less inclined to share publicly after.

2. Identify areas for improvement: By regularly assessing client satisfaction, you can identify areas where your practice may be falling short and make improvements to address those areas - or even specific employees - that are missing the mark. This can help you to enhance the client experience and increase client loyalty over time.

3. Measure the effectiveness of your service delivery strategies: Tracking changes in your NPS over time can help you to measure the effectiveness of your service delivery strategies and initiatives. This information can help you to adjust your approach to better meet the needs of your clients and staff accordingly.

4. Improve customer retention: By regularly assessing client satisfaction, you can identify clients who may be at risk of leaving your business and take proactive steps to retain them.

5. Gain insights into your clients' needs and preferences: The feedback you receive from Net Promoter Surveys can provide valuable insights into your clients' needs and preferences, helping you to better understand their expectations and tailor your offerings to meet those needs.

Finally, the client's individual NPS scores will help inform the likelihood of the client leaving a five-star review. In the sample pipeline above, a client moved to "Case Settled" would inform the client services team of the respondent's NPS score over the course of their engagement. At that time, the team can then determine whether or not to drop the individual into the review request stage triggering the review request workflow in a Review Pipeline.

Here's how the process continues for our clients:

1. Once a case settles, the team moves the client to "Case Closed."

2. The client is removed from the NPS campaign.

3. The client moves to the Client Advocate Pipeline.

By regularly assessing client satisfaction using a measurement like the Net Promoter Score, firms can identify areas where they may be falling short, measure the effectiveness of their service delivery strategies, and take proactive steps to retain clients.

The NPS campaign built into the Law Firm Growth Machine is an excellent example of how to implement an ongoing monitoring system for client satisfaction to safeguard your reputation and drive growth.

Closing Arguments

- The Client Satisfaction Sensor is an ongoing monitoring system that is built into your growth machine and it can help you to maintain the satisfaction of your clients throughout their engagement.

- Assessing client satisfaction using an NPS campaign throughout an engagement can help improve the client experience, avoid negative feedback shared publicly, and provide insights to improve your firm's service delivery.

- The Net Promoter Score (NPS) is a client satisfaction metric that assesses how likely clients are to recommend your firm to others. It can provide valuable insights into areas where improvements can be made, and specifically when to enhance the client experience.

- Regularly assessing client satisfaction through the use of NPS can help you to identify clients who may be at risk of leaving your business and take proactive steps to retain them, improve customer retention, and gain insights into your clients' needs and preferences.

- By routinely assessing client satisfaction, you can identify areas where your practice may be falling short and make improvements to address those areas. This can help you to enhance the client experience and increase client loyalty over time. Additionally, utilizing NPS in your practice can help you to avoid harsh public feedback, measure the effectiveness of your service delivery strategies, and inform the likelihood of clients leaving a five-star review.

"

Nothing influences people more than a recommendation from a trusted friend.

MARK ZUCKERBERG

CHAPTER 11

THE CLIENT ADVOCATE AMPLIFIER

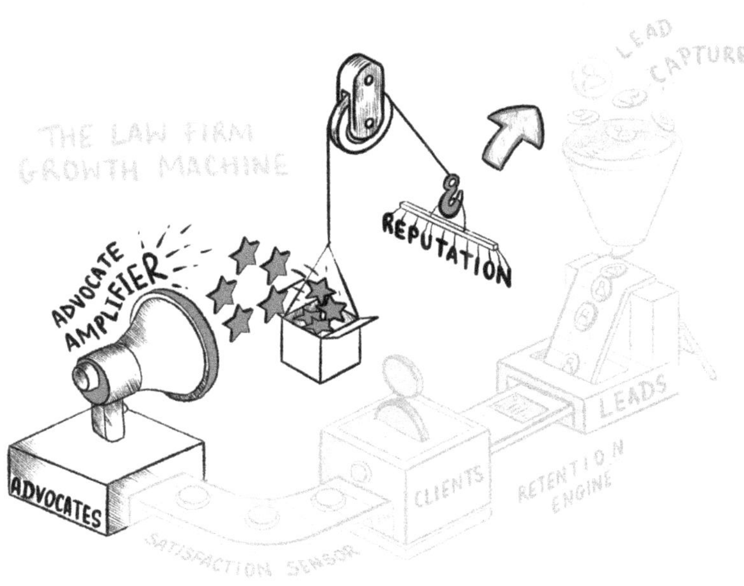

Reviews. For better or for worse, they are necessary, effective, and not going away any time soon. I know you've heard that all before and you're probably thinking, sure - they're important, but who has time for this?!

I've no doubt that despite everything we've discussed regarding your online reputation, boosting your review score online still might not be a high priority.

Our clients are in the very same position.

In fact, we've even acknowledged as much in Chapter 3 - Harsh Realities. You can't do all of this alone. Time and again we have seen how this important task falls to the wayside. However, in response, we've systemized our reputation concepts to eliminate 90% of the work associated with generating reviews, responding to them thoughtfully, sharing them online, and even removing negative reviews.

This system has the power to set your flywheel in motion beginning today. It's our AI-enhanced Client Advocate Amplifier.

Initiate Your System

As you'll recall, marketing dollars are the fuel in your growth machine. That said, online reviews are the lubricant that keeps the gears running smoothly.

If you are new to practice or have recently gone out on your own, positive reviews about your legal acumen, dedication to your craft, commitment to your community, or other personal experiences with you, will still provide prospects with compelling reasons to hire you.

Generating activity in your Google Business Profile Reviews has a near-immediate impact on your firm's visibility and is the fastest way to elevate your profile.

To build momentum, tap into your existing network and leverage those relationships to generate online reviews. If you're an established attorney who is still looking to generate the flywheel effect, I'd bet you have a contact list of former clients that you can reach out to immediately.

Be sure to customize your requests to these various groups - Friends and family, referral partners and colleagues, former clients, and existing clients. You can immediately raise your profile and begin to push the heavy wheel of progress.

The 5Rs to Enhance Reputation

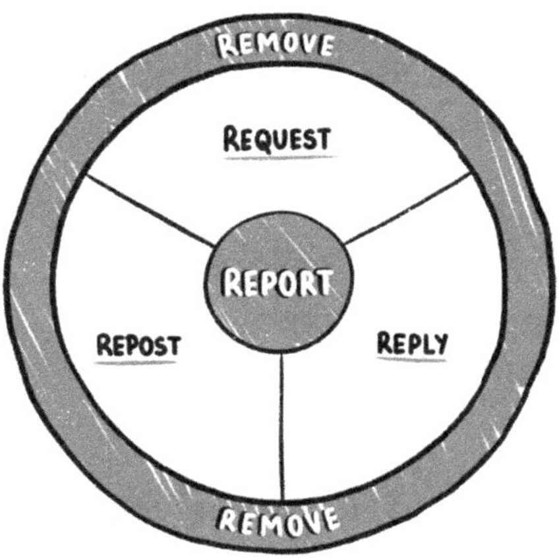

Maintaining, improving, and amplifying your reputation requires that you request reviews, respond to them, and repost positive reviews on Google/social channels. Removing negative reviews should be happening in the background of your Client Advocate Amplifier to protect your reputation whenever possible. Meanwhile, reporting across these areas helps your firm learn how to optimize for even better results. Finally, share your positive client experiences with your referral partners so that they have confidence in your firm's ability to deliver (while giving you still another reason to stay in touch and top of mind).

Here's what you need to do and how you can systemize this approach.

1. Request Reviews

You need to know the right time to ask for a review. As we discussed in the previous chapter, taking an internal measurement of client satisfaction in the way of an NPS (Net Promoter Score) can inform your firm as to the client's likelihood of awarding your firm a five-star review before you make the ask.

Asking once is seldom enough, so if you are serious about generating positive reviews, you'll need multiple requests delivered at various times and through various means until you reach the person when he or she is able to take action.

Having a review request campaign built into an automated delivery system will ensure that the ask is made every time a client is added to the campaign. It will also remove the client from the campaign when they click the link so that you don't pester someone who has in fact taken action. Instead, they will receive only a quick thank you message.

With a review request being as simple as dragging and dropping a prospect into a campaign and knowing with certainty that the system will do the work of consistently making the request, collecting reviews becomes effortless.

Finally, if your requests are not being made via text message, you are inhibiting your likelihood of generating reviews.

2. Reply to all Reviews

Responding thoughtfully to every review will serve your firm well.

No one likes to be ignored, so if a client takes the time to write a review, you need to take the time to respond to the review.

This is a great way to further highlight your personality, your commitment to clients, your interest in their satisfaction, and your gratitude for their feedback.

Remember, you are controlling the narrative around your name.

Responses are also highly valued in the google-verse. If you respond to every review there is twice as much activity on your Google review platform and ample opportunity to highlight your firm's commitment to clients. Both of which Google rewards.

Every review is an opportunity to respond in a way that sells your firm, differentiates you from the competition, and even improves your search engine rankings as reviews are part of the search results algorithm.

That said, including phrases like, "We strive to be the best law firm in Chicago!" will help you rank for terms like "Best law firm in Chicago."

Thankfully, artificial intelligence has transformed our ability to tackle tasks such as this in a way that is thoughtful, personal, and effortless as we will discuss.

3. Repost to All Channels

Your review will live on its original platform such as Google Reviews, but you want to leverage the positive feedback as much as possible by reposting some of those five-star reviews to your business profile, as well as on other channels to generate even more attention.

Creating social media posts out of reviews can be a valuable tool for showcasing your firm, helping to build your reputation, increasing your firm's visibility, boosting confidence on your team, encouraging engagement, and providing that all-important social proof.

Use this as an opportunity to put your brand on blast! Don't just take a screenshot. Use high-quality designs that are on-brand to share what others say about your firm and especially your people. What a wonderful way to celebrate the team and provide them with some well-earned praise in the public square.

And don't forget to tag those posts that mention your wonderful employees to further increase visibility and reach - and earn them some online affection too.

And while not exactly "reposting," be sure you are in fact sharing your five-star reviews with your referral partners - especially those coming from individuals sent to you through that partnership. Doing so will serve several purposes:

First, you'll want your referral partners to have good reason to recommend your firm. If they are privy to your successes they will be confident in making the introduction.

Secondly, saying top of mind is half the battle when it comes to generating referrals. If your referral partners are routinely receiving notice of your satisfied clients and hearing - in their own words - about their experience in working with your firm, they will be more likely to think of you when presented with a referral opportunity.

Finally, sharing client testimonials with your referral partners can foster stronger relationships. They will appreciate the recognition and validation that comes from referring their contacts to a trusted firm. This can encourage referral partners to continue referring clients to you and potentially increase the frequency or quality of their referrals.

Bottom line... share your five star reviews with your referral partners to enhance your reputation and help you generate additional cases.

4. Remove One-Star Reviews

According to Google's review policy, certain types of content such as hate speech, personal attacks, and vulgar language, are prohibited. Yet, according to an industry expert, as many as 70% of negative reviews include this language. And that means you can dispute the review and have it removed.

Removing a single one-star review may not seem like a big deal, but the math shows otherwise. Let's consider a hypothetical example:

Firm A has a total of 50 reviews. 40 of these reviews are five stars and 10 are four stars. This equates to an average of 4.8, a rating any law firm would be proud of.

Now, let's assume the next single review is a one star review. This one review, immediately lowers the average from 4.8 to 4.72.

To regain that 4.8 average, the next 19 reviews need to all be five star reviews.

Conversely, removing that one star review would quickly return the score to 4.8.

But disputing reviews is time-consuming and often goes unaddressed because of other more pressing matters (not to mention failing to have a thorough knowledge of Google's ever-changing and lengthy policies).

Instead of disputing poor reviews, firms typically go to great lengths to avoid getting one-star reviews in the first place, and it's not that this is a bad idea. However, it absolutely must be done properly.

Gating, the tactic of asking a client for feedback (such as thumbs up or thumbs down) before directing clients to a review site (or conversely to a standard feedback form) is against Google policy. And as we've all learned, it really is Google's world. Taking such a risk is truly ill-advised given the outsized power of the platform.

If a law firm violates Google policies, there can be significant risks to its online presence and advertising efforts. Google may penalize the firm by removing their reviews, reducing their search ranking, and even suspending access to Google Ads, all of which can result in a significant loss of business and revenue. Potential clients may also question the firm's trustworthiness if they are known to be in violation of Google policies.

To avoid these negative consequences, you must comply with Google. Focus on providing excellent service, ensuring satisfaction throughout the engagement, regularly assessing that satisfaction, and encouraging all feedback, whether positive or negative, in a way that complies with Google's guidelines, then disputing negative feedback using those very same policies.

I know, I know. You're thinking about the value of time again.

Once more, AI to the rescue! We'll explain.

5. Report Review Data

Finally, like everything we espouse in building a growth system, reporting your review data is a critical element for assessing progress and constantly improving. Your online reviews offer exceptional insight into the market's perception of your brand, your people and your reputation, so tracking and reporting review data is strongly advised.

I'm reminded of a particular client with whom we worked closely on a review strategy and were able to significantly improve their online review scores, directly impacting their visibility in local service ads in particular.

In a year of working with the client and tracking review scores, we had just one 1-star review.

But suddenly something changed. After a six-month streak of rave reviews, the firm amassed six unsolicited one-star reviews in rapid succession.

The precipitous drop in the online reputation score signaled a major breakdown in a particular phase of the engagement that required immediate attention.

That's the good news about bad reviews: They will make you stronger if you choose to learn from them.

For this client, we were able to identify the stage and address the area of concern.

Reporting will also enable you to determine the response rate for your review campaigns.

For example, many law firms can quickly go on Google and tell you how many 1,2,3,4,5 star reviews they have. However, how many can tell you how many cases settled last month, how many of these received a review request, how many left a review request, what the trend in this response rate is, and how many negative reviews were successfully disputed on your behalf?

The trend in the response rate will help you to adjust your language and your approach to further optimize the campaign and thus generate even more reviews.

Eliminating 90% of the Effort

The system for generating reviews can, of course, be implemented manually, but we know that maintaining the system will be challenging - especially for small or solo practices - without the right tools. That's why it's essential to level the playing field by leveraging technology so that you are generating reviews just like those large firms with full-on marketing departments.

It's been my experience that attorneys collect what they consider to be a reasonable number of glowing reviews and then, content with their online presence, they let the initiative wane.

That's not how Google values reviews though, which is exactly why we had to make the system run on auto-pilot.

Google is a living, breathing organism and it likes to be fed a steady diet of reinforcing feedback. When your firm is seen as steadily feeding the beast, they recognize your practice as a thriving contributor worthy of attention. And they reward you for it!

As we mentioned in Chapter 7, your team needs the right tools, and there are powerful tools to support all of these efforts. The challenge always becomes finding, implementing, and training your team to use these tools, not to mention integrating these tools with existing programs to avoid duplicating efforts and mismanaging data.

As James and I recognized the out-sized importance reputation plays in our strategy for generating new business, driving down acquisition costs, and growing a practice, we built an AI-enhanced Client Advocate Amplifier into our system to make effortless work of it all.

Navigating the Client Advocate Pipeline

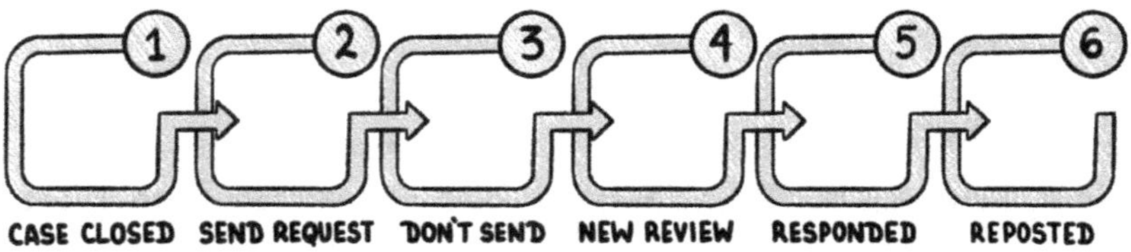

Like the other pipelines in the Law Firm Growth Machine, the Client Advocate Pipeline is overseen by the attorney or staff to track and manage a process. In this case, we are effortlessly managing the process of soliciting feedback, replying to clients, and sharing positive reviews across social channels. Meanwhile, removing negative reviews without requiring any manual action is operating in the background.

Here are the stages of the pipeline and what happens in each.

Stage 1: Case Closed

When a client is moved to Case Closed in the Client Satisfaction pipeline, the client syncs to Case Closed in the Client Advocate pipeline. A member of the team is informed to review the client's NPS score and inquire as to the client's experience.

The team member then makes a determination as to which stage he/she should drag the client to next.

Stages 2 & 3: Send Request or Don't Send Request

At this point, a member of the team, having reviewed previous NPS scores and solicited feedback from the attorney, determines if a review request is advised.

If the client hasn't had a positive experience, the team will drag the client to "Don't Send." I strongly encourage personal outreach if this is the case. Most clients, given the opportunity to express their concerns, will be unlikely to then take their frustrations to the internet. Determine your internal process for ending a client relationship as productively as possible even in the event he or she is unsatisfied.

Assuming the NPS scores and attorney feedback indicate client satisfaction, the client is added to an automated review request workflow in the "Send Request" stage.

Asking for a review once is seldom enough, so if you are serious about generating positive reviews, you'll need multiple requests delivered at various times and through various means until you reach the person when he or she is able to take action.

The text message may look like this:

> *{{contact.first_name}}, this is {{Attorney Full Name}} from {{location.name}}. I'd love to hear about your experience working with my firm. Can you spare 20 seconds to let me know how our team did meeting your needs? I made the same request via email - either link is fine. {{custom_values.review_funnel_trigger}}*
>
> *Thanks in advance - and {{contact.first_name}}, thank you for trusting us with your case.*

Notice that I've included the link to the review platform to make participating effortless.

The email is similar:

New message

To

Subject ***{{contact.first_name}}, do you have a moment?***

Hi {{contact.first_name}},

This is {{Attorney.Full.Name}} from {{location.name}}.

Thank you for trusting us with your case! It has been our pleasure to serve you.

Can you spare 20 seconds to let us know how our team did?

Your feedback is really important to us. It helps us constantly improve and provide folks like you with help when facing the same challenges you've been facing.

It takes only a moment and would mean the world to us. I'll send a follow-up text too - whichever is easiest.

Thanks in advance - and {{contact.first_name}}, thank you for trusting us with your case.

{{Attorney Full Name}}

{{Location Name}}

Note that I let them know it only takes a moment of their time.

Of course, you'll want to be sure you are using technology that informs you the individual has or has not clicked before sending another request, but typically it takes 2 - 3 requests before someone "gets around to it."

Here's what may come next:

New message

To

Subject

Hi {{contact.first_name}}, this is {{Attorney Name}} again. Just wanted to follow up and see if you could spare a moment to let me know about your experience at {{location name}}. Your feedback helps us connect with clients like you who face similar challenges. Thank you in advance!

{{custom_values.review_funnel_trigger}}?

Again, I've added a time commitment and highlighted that they are helping the firm as well as helping others - and the human brain actually thrives on doing things that help others (despite what you see on the nightly news).

A third and final request would be even shorter:

New message

To

Subject

Client, hate to be a pest - last request, I promise! Do you have a moment to click below?

And leave it at that. The final little guilt trip is enough.

A feedback loop into the system ensures that if the link is clicked, no further requests are made.

Stage 4 & 5: New Review and Responded

Stages 4 and 5 are primarily managed in your firm's review dashboard.

When a review is received, it will populate in the "New Review" stage in the Law Firm Growth Machine. Without any additional prompting, Artificial Intelligence (AI) writes a thoughtful, personal, and comprehensive response to the client in a style and tone preferred by the attorney.

The team is notified to review both the client's feedback and the AI-generated response in the dashboard.

If the team determines edits are in order, he or she does so in the dashboard. If the best response is none at all, then no further action is required. If the response is approved in the dashboard, the client moves to "Responded" in the pipeline.

But wait, there's more!

Should that New Review be a five-star review, AI recognizes such and takes that client feedback to create a professionally designed social media post on the firm's branded template. Here too the team member can review the post and approve posting to Facebook, Google Business Profile, and Instagram.

Stage 6: Reposted

When the five-star social post is approved and posted, the client card moves to "Reposted" in the Client Advocate pipeline.

Meanwhile, running in the background all the while, is your Client Advocate Insurance - that's the system that, without any prompting or prodding, is working on your behalf to remove negative reviews by identifying legitimate policy breaches, disputing reviews, and following up relentlessly.

Removal: Running in the Background

As outlined, disputing a negative review can profoundly affect your review score and safeguard your reputation online. The negative experience of an unsatisfied client is the last thing you want a prospect to read when they search for additional information about your firm. Mindful of the impact of social proof, take care to dispute negative reviews, thereby limiting their influence as much as possible.

Of course, not all negative reviews are created equal. Some leave comments, others don't. Some are left by aggravated sale vendors as opposed to clients. Some are ladden with profane language, hate speech, and personal attacks, while others thoughtfully explain their limited experience with your practice.

While we have certainly made the case for a true commitment to a positive client experience, we all know that difficult clients are par for the course, and pleasing everyone over decades of practice is unlikely. In an era of public-shaming and deteriorating politeness (esepcially online), those unhappy individuals may take to public review spaces to air their grievances.

Google has a process in place to dispute reviews, but again these tasks, no matter how important (and they are important), can distract from revenue-generating activities and are often overlooked, especially in smaller firms. We're also keenly aware that remaining abreast of Google's policies and building a strong case to remove a single review is another competency that wasn't covered in your latest by the state bar in your latest continuing education webinar.

That's why we've partnered with a team that focuses on that unique knowledge and skill without having to do anything at all. Our partnership provides our clients with a lovely little insurance policy that runs in the background of The Law Firm Growth Machine and reports back how many negtive reviews are being processed, disputed based on legitimate policy violations (remember, Google's world!), or elevated for additional assessment.

No matter how busy they get, our clients can count on:

- A steady flow of positive reviews that are consistently responded to
- On-brand social posts that provide social proof to prospective clients and engage the community
- Increased visibility
- Insight into how the firm is satisfying clients throughout the engagement

Can you say the same for your firm?

Closing Arguments.

- Despite the outsized importance reviews play in growing a firm, it is still one of the most frequently ignored marketing tasks because of more pressing demands on the firm.

- Firms should implement a system that automates as much of the work as possible to ensure that positive reviews are generated consistently, are used to amplify one's reputation, and require as little as effort as possible.

- An effective Reputation System built using the F5T Framework should enable firms to:

  - Request a review of satisfied clients through a personal and varied approach that may include text, email, and voicemail.

  - Respond to every review in a timely, personal and thoughtful manner.

  - Create on-brand social media posts out of 5-star reviews to increase brand awareness and leverage social proof

Dispute negative reviews using Google policy standards

  - Report review data to improve the client experience and review scores

- Offer unique campaigns for friends, family, colleagues, referral partners, former clients and current clients.

Lawyers can do this work manually, use a variety of tools to lighten the load, or plug into a system such as the one in The Law Firm Growth Machine to consistently deliver results while eliminating 90% of the work associated with the task.

"

The numbers speak for themselves.

MAGIC JOHNSON

CHAPTER 12

THE PULSE

I've always been a little dorky. While I've generally preferred words to numbers, I've often found the magic meaning in numbers to be particularly fascinating. I discovered this passion 25 years ago as a first-year teacher auditing a reading comprehension test for a class of 5th graders. Distressed by my class' poor performance, I created a crude paper and pencil spreadsheet to inform myself as to how many students got each of the questions wrong. I placed a little tally mark to represent each student beside each test question each child answered incorrectly. Sure enough, a pattern arose as to what my students were failing to grasp and where I needed to remediate.

That's the power of data.

Instead of starting all my lessons over or returning to topics that the children already understood, I was able to channel our energies where they were needed most. That insight - the intelligence that came from my test analysis, served my students well. Without wasting time or energy, we focused on specific improvement areas and filled the gaps in our learning.

Fast forward a couple of decades to meeting my business partner James, a former investment analyst who, needless to say, reveled in the world of data. Together, we invested heavily in helping our clients not only systemize their operations but to analyze the data these systems collect. Such data profoundly impacts decision making and has become a cornerstone in how we help law firms to grow.

In fact, after the success we experienced utilizing data in making growth-related decisions, I was called to present a case study on the subject for a group of trial lawyers in the summer of 2021. As I tweaked my slides for the presentation late one night, the Olympics (delayed a full year due to the pandemic) played in the background. A sports anchor was reporting the daily medal count followed by how many world and Olympic records had been broken.

I turned to my husband and said, "I just don't remember breaking records like this all the time in the 80s." I was reminded of the British Cycling team James Clear wrote about in Atomic Habits and realized - data was not only driving us further, the rate at which change occurs is accelerating and further reinforces why you need to take action now.

The Fourth Industrial Revolution, the emphasis of machine learning, artificial intelligence, and data analytics in business, is changing the very nature of work. With the rise of automation, many routine tasks are being taken over by machines, while humans are increasingly being tasked with more complex and creative work. This requires a new set of skills, such as the ability to work with data, understand AI and machine learning algorithms, and collaborate with machines, or at very least compete with those who do.

Of course, the idea that machines have a pulse is an oxymoron. However, we treat The Law Firm Growth Machine as a living phenomenon that can take your law firm to new heights, provided you leverage the insights it is giving you. In fact, you can think of The Pulse as the report generated by an EKG machine – except in this case, EKG doesn't stand for electrocardiogram. It stands for Essential KPIs for Growth!

The Pulse reveals the vital statistics you need to grow. Not only must you take the pulse of the machine, as the CEO, you must keep your finger on this pulse.

The purpose of this chapter is to show you how.

Data-Driven Law Firms

The companies that dominate the headlines today all have something in common - they are data-driven.

After years in a business relationship that was rumored to earn Disney over $300 million annually from Netflix, Disney decided to launch its own streaming service, investing billions, partly because it recognized the tremendous value of learning about its customers by owning and analyzing their data. Meanwhile, Amazon and Netflix cracked the code on enticing customers by sharing what other customers with similar histories enjoyed.

For all these companies, powerful data regarding customer reviews and satisfaction urged users like all of us to watch, try, or buy what was being offered.

This is data at work.

To be data-driven means that you rely on data and analysis to guide decision-making and inform business strategies. It involves collecting, analyzing, and interpreting data to gain insights into prospect behavior, market trends, and operational performance. Being data-driven means that you make decisions based on evidence and facts, rather than intuition or subjective opinions.

Attorneys, conversely, are uniquely trained to think like lawyers. To question. To interpret. To judge. They may be more inclined to rely on subjective factors such as personal experience or expertise, which may not be easily quantifiable or measurable using data.

Attorneys are trained to use legal reasoning and to interpret laws - laws that often deal with complex issues that may not have a clear-cut solution. And attorneys are trained to weigh various factors, such as legal precedent, ethics, and policy considerations, to arrive at a decision. Hardly black and white like data.

It's also been my experience that lawyers are fairly skeptical and always critical thinkers, which can sometimes lead to a healthy skepticism of data. But being data-driven certainly has a place in the legal industry and the firms that will dominate are likely to be the ones that are.

Today data can be used in conjunction with traditional decision-making approaches to make more informed decisions and improve overall performance. It's not about replacing judgment and experience with data, but about using data to enhance and inform these skills.

The Rise of AI in Law

Data and AI are related concepts, but they are not the same thing.

Data refers to the raw facts and figures that are collected and stored by organizations. This data can come from a variety of sources, such as customer interactions, financial transactions, and operational processes. Data can be structured, such as data in a database or spreadsheet, or unstructured, such as data from social media or email messages.

AI, on the other hand, refers to computer systems that can perform tasks that would normally require human intelligence, such as learning, reasoning, problem-solving, and perception. AI systems are trained on data and use algorithms to analyze and interpret that data to make decisions or take actions.

In other words, data is the raw material that AI uses to learn and make decisions. AI systems can analyze and interpret large amounts of data much faster and more accurately than humans, which can help organizations make better decisions and improve their operations.

So, while data is the foundation of AI, AI is the technology that enables organizations to derive greater insights from data and use those insights to improve their business processes and operations.

This is particularly powerful when law firms leverage AI to turn their data into Business Intelligence (BI).

Business Intelligence tools can analyze data and present it in a visually appealing and easy-to-understand format, such as dashboards and reports. This can help law firms to identify key performance indicators (KPIs) and track progress toward goals, such as revenue growth and profitability.

Law Firm Key Performance Indicators

KPIs are measurable values that demonstrate how well your firm is achieving key business objectives—what your firm should be measuring against as signals of achieving success. KPIs are trackable and quantifiable ways to inform the three systems in your firm, which are based on three teams: marketing, intake, and reputation. They also, you'll recall, relate to the F5Ts - Targets and Tracking.

The way to think of KPIs is through feedback loops—the KPI is the origin of the feedback loop. According to Thomas Goetz, "Feedback loops provide people with information about their actions in real time and give them a chance to change those actions, pushing them toward better behaviors."

Let's again consider the goal of weight loss. If the scale is headed in the wrong direction, you know you need to make adjustments. If the scale is headed in the right direction, you may want to double down. Working toward an actual target and measuring that progress will enable you to make better decisions. It also will inspire action among the team if you're headed in the wrong direction.

Identify KPIs that are relevant to your firm and its goals. Good KPIs, long-term as well as short-term goals to provide more immediate feedback, will help fuel your flywheel and keep its momentum going by turning clients into advocates. Focus on 90-day periods, but note that that doesn't mean you can set it and forget it. Remember, a good KPI is measurable and trackable. KPIs should always remain top of mind with your team addressing them regularly and adjusting as needed.

I'll add that seldom do our initial client conversations begin with a lawyer informing me of their KPIs and asking for support in reaching them. Again, most firms fail to have "their numbers" at hand.

The three reasons most people give for their KPI tracking proving to be ineffective are:

1. Measurement isn't automatic,
2. Comparison is irrelevant, and
3. Feedback is slow.

And that's why we make data and reporting so effortless in our growth system.

If you attach the KPI to the components of your flywheel, you know the comparison will be relevant. If you track data on autopilot and get instant feedback, measurement will be automatic and feedback won't be slow.

Essential KPIs

Client Retention KPIs	
Primary KPI = Cases	# of cases screened # of cases retained Source of the cases # of referred cases # of lost cases % of retained cases to screened % of referred cases to screened % of lost cases to screened Cases by Team member Cases by Source Cases by Location Cases by Types Cases by Medium

Client Satisfaction KPIs	
Primary KPI = NPS	NPS score Trend in NPS score # requests # responses Score breakdown Feedback Day(s)/times with highest responses

Client Advocate KPIs	
Primary KPI = Reviews	Average review score Trend in average review score Breakdown of scores Feedback # requests sent # responses sent Day(s)/times with highest responses # 1 stars requested to be removed # 1 stars successfully removed # 1 star removals pending Average time to remove 1 star

Financial KPIs	
Primary KPI = Return on Investment	Total spend Cost per case Average revenue per case Forecasted revenue

The Very Pulse of the Machine

Data in the legal industry is being utilized by independent teams, but seldom are those teams communicating their data with each other in a way that transforms data into intelligence. Again with those darn silos!

By centralizing data, we are able to see how data from one area of the business can be used to inform other areas of the business. Centralizing data so that the marketing team can see what the intake team has achieved, for example, can powerfully affect decisions the marketing team later makes.

You must put technology to good use, using tools that enable data collection to be automated and specifically looking at

a software solution that centralizes all the components you want to track. This will enable you to pull the data together. If you don't have a solution in place that automatically does this for you, you're burdening your staff, the data will be inconsistent and unreliable, the comparison won't be relevant, and feedback will be slow. The goal is to free up your team to do the work that you really want to do and to use the data you've collected to fuel your flywheel and improve your business.

Data is complex but meaning can often be garnered when that data is visualized. Data visualization allows teams to gain insights from complex data sets in a more intuitive and accessible way. Data visualization tools can help organizations identify patterns, trends, and outliers in their data, which can be used to inform decisions. By presenting data visually, it becomes easier for non-technical stakeholders to understand and interpret the information.

Keeping Your Finger on the Pulse

According to a report by IDC and Seagate, the global datasphere, which includes all the data created, captured, and replicated in a given year, was approximately 59 zettabytes (59 trillion gigabytes) in 2020. This is expected to grow to 175 zettabytes by 2025. But collecting data for data's sake is useless.

Once you've collected and visualized your data, you must analyze and utilize it. Revisit your KPIs and the data points with your team regularly, and discuss what's working, what isn't, and what can be done to improve things that aren't trending in the right direction. And don't forget to celebrate wins! Identify what's going well so that others can put those into practice too. Set an agenda to discuss those numbers and take action where necessary.

Here are 4 stages of Data Analysis and an example of how one firm may use this type of analysis at each stage:

1. **Descriptive Analysis** asks the question, *"What happened?"*. It is the simplest type of analytics and the foundation the other types are built on. It allows you to pull trends from raw data and succinctly describe what happened or is currently happening.

   Example: Looking back over the course of the past 12 months, you might notice that opportunities screened, and subsequently case volumes, were highest in Q3 and lowest in Q1.

2. **Diagnostic Analysis** addresses the next logical question, *"Why did it happen?"*. It seeks to identify the root

cause of problems or opportunities, often by comparing different data sets and testing hypotheses.

Example: Seasonality factors could have contributed to a quiet Q1, while your law firm might have made some material changes heading into Q3, such as increasing the marketing budget, adding a new referral partner etc.

3. **Predictive Analysis** asks the question *"What might happen in the future?"*. This stage involves using data to make predictions. It often involves building models that use historical data to identify patterns and make forecasts.

   Example: Based on historical data both in the firm and across the industry, the firm might reasonably forecast ongoing seasonality factors. Meaning Q1 will typically be a softer quarter each year. Despite the addition of the referral partner in Q3, the evidence from marketing campaigns might suggest that the volume of opportunities is more robust in Q3 regardless and therefore the firm should plan accordingly.

4. **Prescriptive Analysis** answers the question, *"What should we do next?"*. It takes into account all possible factors in a scenario and suggests actionable takeaways. This type of analytics can be especially useful when making data-driven decisions.

   Example: The firm needs to determine if investing further in Q3 is advisable. Can the existing team handle the additional volume? Will top intake personnel be available during these months or will vacation play a factor? If staff will be missing, can outsourced options play a role? Similarly, based on the success of the referral partner, a decision might be made to add further referral partners because the net cost is cheaper than the acquisition via digital campaigns.

Despite my data dorkiness, I'm still a words-lover and so I'll leave with you two of my favorites as they relate to keeping a finger on the pulse of your growth machine by centralizing, visualizing and analyzing your data.

First, facts don't care about your feelings. While this is a line largely credited to political commentator Ben Shapiro, it's my partner who taught me to trust the data. Early on as we made decisions about our business, he'd tell me "he doesn't care" what I think - we'll just have to test it. And he's right. In a world of ambiguities it's actually a great relief when something can be distilled down to data points.

And that brings me to my second quote. This one is credited to Jim Barksdale, the CEO of Netscape from 1995 to 1999. Barksdale said, "If we have data, let's look at the data. If all we have are opinions, let's go with mine."

As CEO of your law firm, you can keep that one in your pocket.

Closing Arguments

- We are in The Fourth Industrial Revolution, a period in business that emphasizes the use of data analytics, artificial intelligence, machine learning and automation.

- Data, both structured and unstructured, refers to the facts and figures that are collected within an organization whereas AI refers to computer systems that can perform tasks that would normally require human intelligence, such as learning, reasoning, problem-solving, and perception.

- Lawyers can learn from the most powerful and successful companies in the world. They recognize that utilizing data analytics provides a distinct competitive advantage by enabling them to make decisions that increase efficiency, reduce costs, and identify opportunities.

- Despite its benefits, many firms fail to set targets in the form of KPIs (Key Performance Indicators) citing a lack of efficiency in acquiring their data, poor data quality, and lack of relevance.

- As CEO, lawyers should set KPIs that are relevant to your firm and its goals, relate directly to the elements of the flywheel, are trackable and measurable, and are routinely addressed with the team.

- Firms should use tools that centralize and visualize data so that it can be analyzed in four ways:

- **Descriptive Analysis** - What happened?

- **Diagnostic Analysis** - Why did it happen?

- **Predictive Analysis** What might happen?

- **Prescriptive Analysis** How should I position myself?

✲ Finally, remember that facts don't care about your feelings. In the words of Jim Barksdale, "If we have data, let's look at the data. If all we have are opinions, let's go with mine."

CONCLUSION

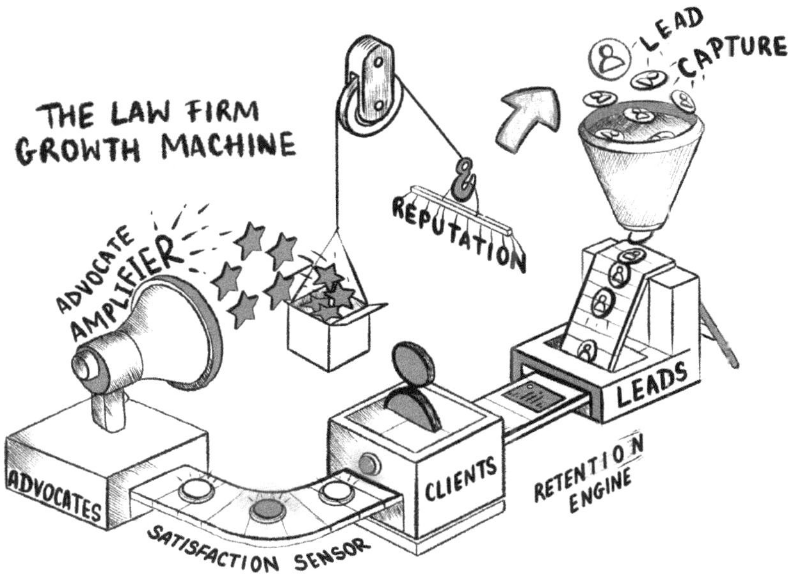

This is personal. With three kids attending, exploring, or considering college, I am deeply frustrated by the fact that a costly education - time-consuming and challenging - can fail to prepare you for the harsh reality of turning that knowledge into income. I'm tired of my many friends and colleagues feeling the stress and strain of their profession. And I'm equally frustrated that Main Street will lose small, dedicated, service-minded attorneys to yet another version of "Big Box" business - like chain restaurants and corporate retailers.

You don't have to be one of them.

I want you to put this plan into place. You have to slow down to speed up - or at least set yourself on cruise control - with the solutions provided on these pages.

Let's recap what you now have as a result of taking this journey together.

In Part 1, we discussed why having a growth machine is so important in today's legal industry. We looked at the challenges facing law firms and how a growth machine can help you survive and thrive in this ever-changing landscape.

I hope I've helped you understand why now is the time to take action and build a growth machine for your law firm. Your ability to succeed and sustain that success will require you to acknowledge these challenges and shift how you operate, just like many of our clients have.

In Part 2, we looked at the strategy at the core of a client-centered, relationship-driven business. This strategy will ensure that investments in your practice are not purely transactional. It will help you achieve the flywheel effect.

We also introduced the Flywheel 5T framework, enabling you to move from strategy to action in your firm by aligning teams, implementing tactics, adopting specific tools, setting targets, and tracking your progress.

We acknowledged the importance of core fundamentals - having a strong brand and the right people, investing in marketing, and adopting a CEO mindset.

At a minimum, every attorney who reads this book will recognize that you must have a strategy for achieving the flywheel effect - a powerful metaphor that I know will continue to influence you as you grow your practice.

Finally, in Part 3, we discussed how to systemize your growth strategy, providing the very inner workings of the machine we have built for clients in firms big and small throughout the country.

We broke down the Client Retention Engine, revealing the pipeline, campaigns, and tactics at the core of our success in converting leads to clients. We invite you to leverage our exact means of converting high-cost leads into high-value clients.

We introduced the Client Satisfaction Sensor, a means of assessing your client's experience to ensure your engagements will help fuel your growth. This system alone can save a client relationship from slipping away, let alone leading to a reputation-crushing negative review.

Next, we lifted the lid on the Client Advocate Amplifier, revealing an AI-enhanced means of building your reputation online while barely lifting a finger! And good thing! Because that finger is firmly on The Pulse. That's the command center for evaluating the health of your firm.

These systems are designed to help you automate routine tasks, capture and convert clients, measure client satisfaction, generate positive reviews, and track your growth KPIs. By leveraging these tools and systems, you can streamline your operations, deliver better value to your clients, and compete with larger firms.

We have provided for you what our custom clients have paid handsomely for over the last five years. These are processes, workflows, tactics, and tips that we have labored over, tweaked, torn apart, tested, optimized, reorganized, and finalized over countless hours. Years.

So what are you going to do with it?

Here's my suggestion.

Start. Start today.

If you are happy with your marketing provider, reputation management, and even case management platforms, I'd suggest you at least introduce to them what you've learned about breaking down silos and aligning platforms to ignite growth. That is an essential first step if you are going to get off the treadmill and start pushing the flywheel.

I'll be honest, getting these platforms aligned will require some heavy lifting on your end, so if time is a commodity you cannot spare, there is an alternative...

Book a free strategy call with me.

We'll discuss where you are with your practice, where you're trying to go and, subsequently, map out the appropriate strategy to achieve those goals.

Even if we never work together, you'll still walk away with a clear plan to achieve your growth goals.

James and I learned early on that the best way to achieve our goals is to help others achieve theirs. We're good at what we do, and if you're good at what you do and ambitious to grow further, we want to be alongside you every step of the way.

ACKNOWLEDGEMENTS

A part of me has been writing the acknowledgments to my book since I'm a little girl. Granted, I never imagined it would be a book related to law firms, growth, or business, but it still never would have happened without the people who have deeply and significantly influenced me since then, and none more so than my parents.

It is no doubt that their love, guidance, good nature, and support steadied a foundation from which I could grow. I am eternally grateful for the values my mom and dad instilled in my siblings and me and the big, beautiful tapestry of extended family and friends we were surrounded by. They gave us an education, a life worth aspiring to for our own families, and the will to work for it.

My dad will undoubtedly hold this book in his hand, marvel at it, smile proudly, and ask, "Did you trace this?"

Though I have written many, many New Year's resolutions to be more like Christie, I am actually the older sister. She has played maid of honor in every instance of my life and I can think of no one more generous in that role. She has stood by me through life's highest highs and my lowest lows and has probably gotten more than she bargained for. She's still someone I strive to be more like. Heck, we all should.

I'm grateful that my experiences over the last several years have brought me closer to my brother Tim. I have long admired his entrepreneurial spirit and have relished the opportunities to share this journey with him.

Three women helped shape my sense of self outside the home – Karen Carpentieri, Jenni Ihm and Kathleen Perry. To Aunt Karen – you made work look glamorous and something I wanted to be a part of while the other (equally important!) women in my life were graciously breading chicken cutlets. Jenni, you gave me the voice and authority to quite literally command a stage, and I am so grateful for the gift of your trust in me at such a very young age. You taught me so much. And Ms. Perry – to this day, when my footfalls are fast and firm with the confidence of an independent woman, it is the echo of your steps in the hall that I hear.

Over the last decade I have had the gift of amazing people who believed in me more than I believed in myself. Claire, John, Mark, Chip, Chris, Michael, Joel & Kristen... your confidence in me pushed me to learn more, do more, work more, and be more, always desperate to deliver. I hope you feel I have.

There are so many lawyers and professionals working in the legal industry that have (perhaps unwittingly) become part of our story – Arnie, Maddy, Brad, Gary, Seth, Byron, EJ, Dean, Ken, Nalini, Paul (both of you!), Jason, Rob, Brooke, Pam, Chris, Lindsay... and countless others. We thank them for sharing their insights, expertise and friendship. It just keeps getting better.

I am also incredibly grateful to the extraordinary talents of those who quite literally pulled this book together with me:

eagle-eyed Trevin Jacobson, artist-extraordinaire Sheoli Chaturvedi, designer and typesetter Jenni Woodhead, and the amazing Tina Konstant. Thank you for the invaluable ways you've contributed to making this book a reality.

To my children – Jules, Holden & Coby Jane... Gosh, I love you. I know this period of time has been one in which I have been far busier than you may have liked, but there have been so many upsides that I hope you will recognize in time.

First, you are capable and resilient. You didn't NEED me to find that sock or make that sandwich, and that's not to say you wouldn't have liked me to, but I know this experience has made you more prepared for the world you will enter.

I hope you see in me the example that I desperately seek to model for you:

Work hard.

Be dependable.

Deliver on your promises.

Accept that things may not come easily or feel worth it, but fortune often favors those who simply keep showing up. This simply cannot be said without mention of Uncle Billy who I so wish could be here to celebrate this accomplishment. He would be so proud.

Most importantly, kids, choose your partner wisely.

I have been lucky to have the backing of two men on this journey: A great business partner and an amazing husband.

James is the first person I have worked with who sought to tap my strengths not to build his own empire, but to help me build mine. He is humble, talented, and intimidatingly hard-working. He challenges me in ways that I often despise and always appreciate. Eventually.

And my life partner, my husband of more than 22 years, Chris. Well... simply put, none of this is possible without you. I no longer know where I end, and you begin. You are all the things I am not myself – the logic to my instinct, the contented to my restless, the patience to my impulsivity. You fill the gaps that make it possible to be me in this life we share, and I cannot imagine living it without you. I have never had someone believe in me more, champion me with such enthusiasm, or love me so fiercely. Except my grandma. Who would have endlessly boasted of this book (even if Grandpa would have been the only one to actually read it).

GLOSSARY

Abandoned: A lead or prospect who is not qualified or whom the firm chooses not to retain.

Acquisition: The process of acquiring new leads and clients.

Activation: The process of engaging leads and encouraging them to take the next step in connecting with the firm.

Artificial Intelligence: Technology that enables machines to perform tasks that normally require human intelligence, such as language processing or decision-making.

Auto Follow-Up Campaign: Series of text, email, and voicemail messages delivered to leads with whom the firm has yet to connect with by phone.

Awareness: The extent to which potential clients are aware of the law firm's existence and services.

Booking Widget: A tool that allows prospects to schedule consultations or appointments directly through the law firm's website.

Brand: The identity and reputation of the law firm as perceived by its clients and the public. The collective opinion of the public as to the firm's value promise.

Campaign: A focused, targeted marketing initiative designed to achieve a specific goal, such as generating leads or increasing brand awareness.

CEO: Chief Executive Officer - the highest-ranking officer in a company responsible for overall strategy and decision-making.

Chatbot: An automated chat program that can interact with website visitors and answer frequently asked questions.

Client Centered: A philosophy that puts the client's needs, preferences, and values at the center of all business decisions and interactions.

CMS: Case Management System - a software platform used to create and manage legal cases.

Conversion: The process of turning leads into clients.

Cost Per Acquisition (CPA): The cost of acquiring a new client.

CRM: Customer Relationship Management - software used to manage interactions with prospects, leads, and clients.

CTA: Call to Action - a prompt designed to encourage a specific action, such as filling out a lead form.

Data: Information collected to inform decision-making and improve performance.

Digital Natives: A generation of individuals who have grown up using digital technology and are comfortable with using it to communicate, interact, and perform tasks.

Flywheel: A metaphor for the momentum generated by consistent, small efforts that compound over time to produce unstoppable momentum.

Fourth Industrial Revolution: The current era of technological advancement characterized by the integration of cyber-physical systems, the Internet of Things, and other emerging technologies that are transforming the way we live and work.

GMB/GBP: Google My Business/Google Business Profile - a free tool that allows businesses to manage their online presence on Google.

KPI: Key Performance Indicator - a measurable value that indicates how well a company is achieving its goals.

Lead: A person who has shown interest in the law firm's services and provided their contact information.

Lead Form: A form that captures a prospect's contact information and other relevant details.

Lead Magnet: A free resource or offer provided on the website designed to attract leads and encourage them to provide their contact information.

Lost: A prospect who has chosen not to hire the law firm despite our ability to serve them.

Machine: A highly optimized system that runs smoothly and efficiently, often through automation and the use of technology, to make work easier.

Mission: The overarching purpose or reason for the law firm's existence, often communicated through a mission statement.

NPS: Net Promoter Score - a measure of customer loyalty and satisfaction.

NPS Campaign: A series of text and/or email messages designed to collect a measurement on a current client's level of satisfaction.

Post Call Follow-Up Campaign: Series of text, email, and voicemail messages delivered to a prospect the firm has spoken with and can help but who has not yet signed a retainer.

PPC: Pay-Per-Click - a form of digital advertising in which the advertiser pays each time their ad is clicked.

Pipeline: A sequence of steps that a prospect or client goes through on their journey from being at one stage to another.

Review Request Campaign: A series of text and email messages designed to solicit a five-star online review from the client.

ROI: Return on Investment - the measure of profitability resulting from an investment.

SEO: Search Engine Optimization - the practice of optimizing website content and structure to improve its ranking in search engine results.

Strategy: A plan of action that outlines how the law firm will achieve its goals and objectives. A way to win.

System: A network of coordinated processes, tools, and technologies that enable the law firm to consistently and efficiently carry out operations.

Printed in the USA
CPSIA information can be obtained
at www.ICGtesting.com
LVHW021643120624
783016LV00001B/86

9 798218 173289